QUILTER'S ACADEMY

Vol. 5—Master's Year

A Skill-Building Course in Quiltmaking

Harriet Hargrave & Carrie Hargrave-Jones

C&T PUBLISHING

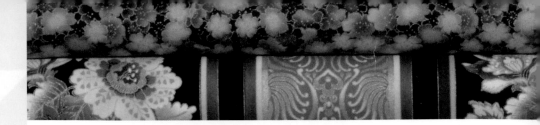

Text and photography copyright © 2015 by Harriet Hargrave and Caroline Jones

Artwork copyright © 2015 by C&T Publishing, Inc.

Publisher: Amy Marson

Creative Director: Gailen Runge

Art Director / Cover Designer: Kristy Zacharias

Editor: Carrie Hargrave-Jones and Harriet Hargrave

Book Designer: Kristen Yenche

Production Coordinator: Zinnia Heinzmann

Production Editor: Alice Mace Nakanishi

Illustrator: Kirstie Pettersen

Photography by Brian Birlauf, unless otherwise noted

Published by C&T Publishing, Inc., P.O. Box 1456, Lafayette, CA 94549

Library of Congress Cataloging-in-Publication Data

Hargrave, Harriet.

Quilter's academy : a skill-building course in quiltmaking / by Harriet Hargrave and Carrie Hargrave.

p. cm.

ISBN 978-1-57120-594-0 (softcover)

1. Patchwork. 2. Quilting. I. Hargrave, Carrie, 1976- II. Title.

TT835.H3384 2009

746.46--dc22

2009008787

Printed in the USA

10 9 8 7 6 5 4 3 2

A Course in Quilting

A fresh new approach to uncovering the details that make quilting fun and rewarding. As we progress, you will be challenged to make stunning quilts using the skills achieved in earlier courses.

Quilting 501—Master's Year

Your master's year brings everything you have learned in *Volume 1—Freshman Year* through *Volume 4—Senior Year* together. You are entering into the world of medallion quilts, a style of quilts that can be anything you want them to be, from very formal to very simple or heavily quilted to simple and everyday. Medallion quilts were in their glory during the latter part of the eighteenth century and reappear in the quilt world time and again. This is not so much a pattern book as a book of inspiration and the culmination of all the knowledge you have achieved through the *Quilter's Academy* courses. We have approached the quilts as a way of analyzing and troubleshooting piecing situations, and how to find the solutions. We hope that you gain a real appreciation for these quilts and put all your skills into creating an original one of your own by the end of the book.

Note from the Authors

This has been a difficult book to write. We didn't want it to be a pattern book, but a book to inspire quilters to create original medallion-style quilts using all the skills that have been taught in the previous four volumes of *Quilter's Academy*. *Volume 5* is the culmination of all the techniques and the lessons in drafting and math, as well as the precision we have taught in this series. This is the master's plan, where you should be able to apply all your knowledge into critical thinking and original design. We have approached this book from different directions. Carrie has always been excited to start with a blank sheet of graph paper, a stack of fabrics, and her huge box of colored pencils and let all that speak to her. It leads her into original quilts inspired by many different things. Her skills allow her to be fearless when it comes to the settings and piecing, as she is confident that she will be able to work out any problems. Harriet, on the other hand, has a passion for antique quilts and tends to collect orphans that are damaged or totally worn out. Her favorite thing is to bring these beauties back to life using modern techniques and new fabrics, but still getting the look and feel of a 175-year-old quilt. So, we have combined both of our styles to present a book to you that approaches quilt design from several angles. Harriet is taking you on a journey of working out the math and dimensions when working with a very old quilt, or from a photograph of an antique quilt. Carrie is working from her own original designs, new fabrics, and a more modern look to her quilts, but still in the medallion style. We sincerely hope you will jump in with both feet and utilize all the ideas to create your own masterpiece!

The authors take full responsibility for the contents of this book, including the technical accuracy of the information. Please direct any questions to quilt.academy.q.a@earthlink.net. Please visit the Quilter's Academy blog, too, for additional information and discussions: quiltersacademy.blogspot.com.

Contents

Dedication

This volume of *Quilter's Academy* is dedicated to Izzie, Harriet's furry kitty companion of almost twelve years. From the time she was little and came to live with us, Izzie was in the studio. There wasn't a quilt made that she didn't enjoy as much as we did. She never met a quilt she didn't like, and her favorites were the most valuable antique ones.

She was pictured as a kitten in *Heirloom Machine Quilting* in 2004, as she rode on the quilt while Harriet quilted it. She learned from the beginning that quilting is fun. Her life ended during the writing of this book, so we thought it an honor to her to dedicate this book to her.

We share this dedication with all the furry quilting companions of all types that quilters have enjoyed and lost. There is a big empty spot in the studio, but one of the others is in training and it is looking good. God bless all the animal companions that have such a huge place in our hearts. We will always miss you, Izzie.

Izzie helped write every book.

Quilts and kitties—what could be better?

Preface

The human mind craves challenges, and we have tried to create and develop this way of thinking through the first four books. This book is going to put all the skills and ideas developed in the previous books into play. Medallion quilts can be quite a challenge and are not the style of quilt that is made in a weekend.

When perusing recently published (within the past fifteen years) books dealing with medallion quilts, we found that they mainly amounted to pattern books, not manuals that teach you how to develop and design your own medallion.

This train of thought has put us in the difficult position of trying to find a way to write about the analytical thinking processes that are involved in planning these quilts. There are so many different ways to approach them, and we wanted to cover as many of these ideas as we could.

So, we came up with a plan to design some modern-looking medallions using the first four books as guidelines, keeping the piecing simple at first, then developing ideas and thoughts for more complex design as we went. Carrie designed quilts working from inspiration photos that utilized all the skills she has mastered through the writing of the first four volumes of *Quilter's Academy*. This approach led Harriet into dissecting wonderful antique medallions and working out the piecing sizes through drafting and lots of calculator work. Then she decided to work from photos of quilts that live in museums that we don't have access to. This led to a gallery of borders that we found in dozens of quilts that we studied, as well as outline drawings for you to use as a template for your own original medallions.

We hope you find this book exciting and that it inspires you to take the time to create your own masterpiece. This is your master's degree year, so it deserves the time and attention that you would give an advanced degree. Sit back, enjoy the journey, and create something wonderful.

A Note from Harriet:
I want to congratulate Carrie for hanging in there with me to this level of skill. When we started the series she was a new student of quiltmaking—a self-proclaimed "topper." I have watched her dedication to excellent workmanship and learning, even though she really didn't want to be a quilter. Not only has she made half the quilts in all the books, but she has designed many, pieced them all, and beautifully machine quilted all of her tops. Her quilts in this book show the dedication she shows for learning and achieving the highest standards in her work. I hope she is an inspiration to our readers to follow suit.

Introduction

This is the fifth book in the *Quilter's Academy* series. Our mission has been to write a series of books that teach the basics while at the same time trying to instill a desire in our students to create original quilts. We feel that the art of classic quiltmaking is being left behind for the quick and easy "modern" quilting fad. The problem with keeping everything fast and simple is that eventually you will get bored with the results. We hope that that starts to create a desire for a challenge. Now the problem becomes evident that few skills have been learned in the making of more simple, modern quilts, so there is a lack of knowledge as to how to start making the more difficult patterns. We sincerely hope that this series has helped people realize that there is no substitute for good workmanship, whether the pattern is simple or complex. Easy is not always best. It seems our society is reaching a point of chronic mediocrity and quilting is going along for the ride. Many quilters would argue that it is just about having fun and getting things done quickly, that techniques are completely subjective and there are no hard and fast rules. We understand how you can be sucked into that thought process. However, as in all things in life, the reality is that there is a need for a toolbox of skills to be able to progress. Not all quilts need to be masterpieces, but with a great skill set, you can make anything you desire, and make it well.

If you are just discovering the *Quilter's Academy* series, please don't judge it based on the photos of the quilts. We have kept the fabric choices very traditional to keep them from looking dated, which the use of faddish colors can do. We do hope that you realize that all the patterns can be jazzed up by using wild and crazy fabrics, just as they can look very traditional by using more subtle prints and colors. The only thing keeping your projects from turning out like you want is your imagination and a little planning and doing mock-ups.

We also want to remind you that you have been tested throughout the series by the "mistakes" we have in the books. Some were editing oversights and some were placed there deliberately. Our intention was to cause you to think through the problem and arrive at the answer by applying all you had learned up to that point, much like a midterm exam. We knew that if we had put "tests" throughout the book, most readers would just skip over them. We have received all types of comments and emails concerning this. Some were angry, some were very judgmental toward us personally, and some commented that they could work out the answer because they had learned from the previous lessons and classes and could apply the knowledge. *Yeah!!!* These students totally got it! We hope you were one of those readers! If so, you are now ready for this next challenge.

Class 510

There are four generally accepted types of geometric quilts: block quilts, striped or strip quilts, allover quilts, and quilts with a dominating central pattern, known as *framed* or *medallion* quilts. *Volumes 1–4* of the *Quilter's Academy* series dealt with block-, strip-, and allover-style quilts. *Volume 5* is leading you into the exciting world of medallions.

> Me-dal-lion \me-'dal-yen\ n 1: a large medal.
> 2: something resembling a large medal; esp.:
> a tablet or panel in a wall or window bearing
> a figure in relief, a portrait, or an ornament

Webster's definition of a medallion explains why "medallion" quilts are so named. A medallion quilt is known for having an ornamental center pattern (panel) surrounded with borders. The medallion (also called *center-square* or *framed* pattern) is one of the earliest pieced-work formats, and was popular in both America and England during the late eighteenth and early nineteenth centuries. Medallions were one of the earliest styles of quilts made in early America, as early colonists brought the tastes and fashions of their home countries with them. The dictates of English taste were followed by the upper classes in clothing and home furnishings until the early 1800s. After the eighteenth century, American and English quilt styles diverged, the English staying with the medallion quilt style and the Americans going on to predominantly the block style that we still see most often today. As you study the progression of the medallion quilt, you see that the borders began to change with time. As more borders became solid or printed fabric, and pieced

and unpieced borders were alternated, more patterns were created for the pieced sections. These patterns were eventually recast as blocks to form the quilt's entire overall design. Quilting became less and less significant, as ornate quilting would have been lost in the busyness of the fabrics. Many of the quilts were tightly quilted in simple patterns such as parallel diagonal lines and diamonds.

Averil Colby wrote in her book *Patchwork*:

> "A type of quilt design that has no traditional name in this country (England) but the description 'framed' may serve to classify a large number of quilts in which the characteristic of the design is a planned centre-piece surrounded by a series of borders or 'frames'. These patterns are not peculiar to any district and have been popular in poor as well as better class work. The centre panels are carried out in all-appliqué or all-geometric patterns or a combination of both or even a piece of printed cotton; the outline may be oval, round, rectangular or square and the squares are often put in diamond-wise." *

> The Orlofsky's state: *"Medallion quilts tended to be more formal in their beginning. When today's quilters think of old quilts, they may be going back only as far as the 1930s. Quilting has been around in one form or another before history was recorded. When the colonists arrived in America, there is little known about whether they brought quilts with them or not, but as the colonies were settled the "making of quilts provided a more creative outlet for the entire family and produced one of the few flamboyant elements of color and style in an otherwise utilitarian household." ***

* *Averil Colby, Patchwork, Charles Scribner's Sons, New York, 1958, page 60*

** *Patsy and Myron Orlofsky, Quilts in America, Abbeville Press, New York, 1974, page 29*

Examining the textiles that early quilts were made from, we look to the textiles used for clothing and home furnishings:

> *"The colonists were not obliged to confine themselves to homespun materials. On the contrary, their contact with England assured them a constant supply of foreign fabrics."* ***

*** *Frances Little, Early American Textiles, Century Company, New York, 1931, page 223*

The history of the development of the textile industry in America is fascinating and well documented. The women living along the Eastern Seaboard had access to goods coming in from Europe, if they could afford them. The availability was limited, though, and they were expensive. Access to the Eastern Seaboard was crucial, so pioneers in the remote areas west of the coast had to depend largely on their home-loomed fabrics. The fabrics and colors used in colonial quilts were representative of the dress fabrics of the time. Leftover household furnishing fabrics were also apparently used. If you ever get a chance to examine very early nineteenth-century quilts, you will be amazed at the beauty of the fabrics that were used to create them.

The Origins of Medallion Quilts

The generally accepted original source of the design for center-panel medallion quilts was the Indian palampore. Palampores were a single large chintz printed panel used as coverlets for beds. They came before quilts appeared, before the end of the seventeenth century.

Whole Cloth Palampore. Collection of Winterthur Museum

These pieces were discovered by traders as early as the 1500s when the route around the Cape of Good Hope was discovered. As this fabric slowly made its way to Europe, much interest developed, as it was unlike anything people there had ever seen before. The fabric became known as *chintz*. Today we think of chintz as a glazing process to give luster to the surface of fabrics. In India, the name represented painted or printed cloth, some of which was glazed. The early designs were made to please Islamic trading partners with India.

In *Origins of Chintz*, the authors described what palampores looked like:

> *"The characteristic 17th century palampore [and quilt] designs comprised a central medallion and four related corner motifs on a flowery field surrounded by a wide border. The ultimate source of the medallion and corner motifs was probably the Persian manuscript cover, which may also be said to have inspired the same elements in Persian carpet-design."**

* *John Irwin and Katherine B. Hall Origins of Chintz Her Majesty's Stationery Office, London, 1970*

There is reference to quilts in the same document as palampores, referring to pieces that were already quilted. The term *quilt* was used in its true sense of a padded coverlet. In the book *Origins of Chintz*, quilts were referred to as "stuffed with cotton, painted and patterned exceedingly prettily." Quilts were recorded to be stitched in India before being exported, but the Indian fabrics were also professionally quilted in England.

These fabrics and quilts were first brought into England in the early 1600s. Once a shipping route to India was established, each ship that returned to England would bring a few quilts and pieces of cloth. They became a huge commodity, as fabrics made in England and Europe during this period were not painted or printed cotton. At this same period in time, English calico printers had mastered the technique of block printing but only in a limited range of colors: brown, black, purple, and red. The fabrics from India were alive with brilliant colors and fantasy through naturalistic movement and floral forms. These fabrics were to become a great influence on English and American quilt design.

By 1643, the fabrics were so popular that the English started to request that the fabric conform more to the European taste, with a lighter ground instead of the "sad" red grounds that didn't please all the buyers. In 1700, a prohibition in England forbade the importation, use, and wear of East India fabrics. This caused the English printers to start imitating the Indian goods. By 1754, it was hard to distinguish between the English and Indian printed goods. All of this just led to more demand.

The high cost of importing Indian fabrics, the ban and consequent reduction of trade with India, and the French Revolution caused chintz fabric to be very expensive and not always readily available during the 1700s. This is thought to be what led women of the eighteenth century to make quilts using the Tree of Life design along with bouquets of flowers surrounded by borders to get the "look" of the Indian palampore. Women had been doing elaborate embroideries on sturdy fabric, then cutting them out and appliquéing them onto finer fabric such as velvet or silk. They used their embroidery and appliqué techniques to create the look of Persian embroidery, called *resht* work. This was a process of cutting out pieces of fabric and applying them to different colored backgrounds. The coming together of all these processes is what we now call *Broderie Perse*.

Counterpane, 1782 (Philadelphia), appliquéd in palampore style.
Collection of Winterthur Museum

The following quilt is a much simpler appliqué quilt, relying on fine quilting to fill two plain borders. It appears that one or a couple of similar multicolored block-printed fabrics were used for the Broderie Perse appliqué. The outer appliquéd frame is an excellent way to finish a more simple-style medallion.

Robison Crusoe 1790–1820,
by Frances Brook, Valentine Museum, Richmond, Virginia

The medallion style was taken into another realm with the appliquéd medallion below. This style was typical of quilts in Maryland and Virginia at the turn of the nineteenth century. The appliqué on the following quilt did not rely on a printed fabric for design.

Framed medallion, 1794–1817 (northern Virginia), by Martha Harness.
The Daughters of the American Revolution Museum, Washington, D. C.

At the behest of Benjamin Franklin, a young English calico printer, John Hewson, came to Philadelphia to set up a calico-printing business. It is said that it is nothing short of miraculous that the business survived from 1774 into at least the early 1820s. Due to his business's being almost destroyed during the Revolution, he had to resort to changing his dyeing methods to the resist style. By 1780, he had built his business back and could again print with a full range of colors. He is known for the counterpane below. This was block printed as a whole piece.

John Hewson Counterpane, 1780 (Philadelphia).
Collection of Winterthur Museum

By the late 1700s, we start to see piecing incorporated into the medallion style.

Tree of Life, 1820, very little Broderie Perse, more piecing and quilting.
The Daughters of the American Revolution Museum, Washington, D. C.

The exclusive use of printed fabric changes the look of medallion quilts. Amazing chintz florals and stripes were available, and using them as borders allowed for the frugal use of expensive fabrics.

Framed medallion quilt, 1825–1835, each border using flamboyant patterned fabric. The Daughters of the American Revolution Museum, Washington, D. C.

Knowing the history of the medallion quilt style is important, as Indian textiles furnished the basics of design for the American and English center-medallion pieced and appliquéd quilts that were so popular at the end of the eighteenth century. This style then led in part to the block-style quilt.

In the early days of quiltmaking in America, there were three basic types of quilts: the wholecloth quilt, the high-style central medallion, and the mosaic piecework style. The Indian palampore tended to have borders and corners with regularly arranged design elements, which are thought to be one direct link to the block-style quilts we see later. The second link to block-style quilts was the continuous mosaic pieced quilts so popular in England. This transition from appliquéd central medallions to early mosaic quilts is referred to by one quilt historian as

> *"A basic design of a repeat block jammed together with others of its kind and arranged helter-skelter."* *

* Jeannette Lasansky, In the Heart of Pennsylvania Symposium Papers, Oral Traditions Project of the Union County Historical Society, Lewisburg, PA, 1986, page 21

It is thought that the two design ideas eventually joined in the overall block style so common today. By the early 1800s, medallion-style quilts started to become more about piecing than appliqué and quilting. Pieced versions of the center medallion style were made primarily between 1820 and 1840, using numerous small pieces of cloth left over from clothing, curtains, or bed hangings. Fabrics from the turn of the eighteenth century to the first quarter of the nineteenth century can be found in one quilt, making them the ultimate scrap quilt and a quilt collector's dream, a true library of fabrics of the time period.

Unfinished pieced bedcover, 1790–1800, 54" × 55",
Courtesy of Mount Vernon Ladies' Association of the Union

Framed medallion, 1840, Virginia Quilt Museum

Fast forward to the twentieth and twenty-first centuries.

Blue center square-in-a-square medallion, 1940, from Harriet's collection

Ray of Light, 1977, 84" × 94", by Jinny Beyer

Blue Medallion, 1984, 64" × 84", by Harriet Hargrave

Through an Open Window, 2006, 87" × 85",
designed and quilted by Lorie Stubbs, Lakewood, Colorado

Wholecloth quilts are a type of medallion style. They generally have a center design that is then surrounded by one or more elaborately quilted borders. Although not an actual medallion, these types of quilts are a very close relative.

Tribute to Barbara, 2013, 70″ × 70″, designed by Barbara Chainey, quilted by Harriet Hargrave

We hope this journey through the history of these quilts has been an inspiration. As you have seen, the idea of the medallion quilt can be translated into a myriad of forms and contain several different techniques and skills. If any of this information piques your interest in the history of textiles, or the pursuit of more photos of quilts of these eras, we have included a bibliography of the books we used and have in our library. This list is the tip of the iceberg, as there is no way we can list the over 200 titles Harriet has in her collection that contain quilt history and/or medallion quilts. The books listed have their own bibliographies that will take you into the nether regions of your city library or on an extensive Internet search. Another wonderful source of images is quiltindex.org. There you will find photographs of the quilt collections of many museums. Happy hunting!

Bibliography

Bacon, Lenice. *American Patchwork Quilts*. New York: William Morrow & Co., Inc., 1973.

Beyer, Jinny. *The Art and Technique of Creating Medallion Quilts*. McLean, Virginia: EPM Publications, Inc., 1982.

Eaton, Linda. *Quilts in a Material World*. New York: Abrams, 2007.

Irwin, John, and Katherine B. Hall. *Origins of Chintz*. London: Her Majesty's Stationery Office, 1970.

Kiracofe, Roderick. *The American Quilt*. New York: Clarkson Potter Publishers, 1993.

Little, Frances. *Early American Textiles*. New York: The Century Co., 1931.

Montgomery, Florence. *Printed Textiles, English and American Cottons and Linens 1700–1850*. New York: The Viking Press, 1970.

Orlofsky, Patsy, and Myron Orlofsky. *Quilts in America*. New York: McGraw Hill Book Co., 1974.

Peto, Florence. *American Quilts and Coverlets*. New York: Chanticleer Press, 1949.

Pettit, Florence. *America's Printed and Painted Fabrics 1600–1900*. New York: Hastings House, Publishers, 1970.

Prichard, Sue. *Quilts 1700–2010: Hidden Histories, Untold Stories*. London: V&A Publishing, 2010.

Pullen, Martha. *Historic Quilts of the DAR Museum*. Birmingham, Alabama: Hoffman Media, 2011.

Safford, Carleton L., and Robert Bishop. *America's Quilts and Coverlets*. New York: E.P. Dutton & Co., 1972.

Schoeser, Mary, and Celia Rufey. *English and American Textiles from 1790 to the Present*. New York: Thames and Hudson, 1989.

Class 520

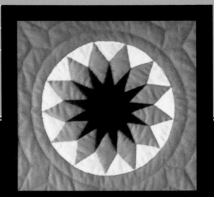

When you see a well-designed medallion quilt, it is awe-inspiring. When the center "medallion" and all the borders work well with each other, the end result is a true attention grabber. However, if the elements of the quilt design are not well thought out, it might grab your attention, but not for the enjoyment of viewing it. The problem areas are distracting. A border that is not the correct scale for the position it is in, or poorly fitted, can ruin the entire project. A fabric that is too bold for its position in a border, or a poorly planned corner treatment, can also disarm the viewer. Elements within the quilt that draw attention to themselves tend to take away the enjoyment of unity that is the goal of a well-executed medallion quilt.

A medallion quilt in its most basic definition consists of an interesting center area surrounded by a series of various borders. What you choose to be the center of the quilt should be something interesting enough to hold its own with the many borders that will surround it. For all the work that will go into the making of the quilt, you want the final project to be stunning.

The center is traditionally a wholecloth panel, a pieced block, or an appliquéd block. *Broderie Perse* (a technique where cutout shapes are appliquéd to the background) was often used to combine different elements from different printed fabrics to create an interesting center. What style your quilt will take on depends on what the center consists of and what kind of borders you choose to add. Planning a medallion gets easier as you do it. Choosing the center generally leads the way for where the rest of the quilt will go. Because it is the focal point, it sets the stage for what follows.

When thinking about the style of quilt you want to work on, you might want to analyze the look of medallions that appeal to you and the elements those quilts include, and make note if they have these elements:

❋ Heavy and complicated pieced borders

❋ Simple borders using just the fabric design

❋ Appliqué in a border, just the center, or not at all

❋ Built-in areas for elaborate quilting

❋ A look of elegance and/or antiquity

❋ A very modern and sophisticated look

❋ A very scrappy design or a planned palette of fabrics

❋ A soft and subtle or loud and noisy feel

Once you have thought about what you want the quilt to look like, you will have a good idea of what kind of fabrics will help you achieve your goal. If you are at a loss as to where to start, do some research and study the many photos of medallions from museum collections. These will help in getting a mental image as to how busy you may want to make your quilt, color combination ideas, border ideas, and so on. You might also be inspired by the vast number of border ideas in Class 590. This is not a quilt to rush. These tend to talk to you as you design or construct them, so be open to changing your direction if things aren't turning out as you planned. Your quilt and you are entering into a working relationship.

If you take the time to do research of past medallion styles, you will find a great deal of variety. As we discussed in Class 510, the styles of medallions have evolved over time because of the fabrics available as well as the places they were made. Up until the 1980s, medallion quilts were mainly based on the traditional English style. In 1982, Jinny Beyer released her book *The Art and Technique of*

Creating Medallion Quilts. This book sent the quilt world into a period of revived interest in medallion-style quilts. The difference this time around was that the quilts took on a very coordinated look through the use of fabrics that Jinny Beyer designed specifically for the purpose of making quilts with many borders that all coordinated. The use of elaborately pieced blocks for the center medallion, in many different shapes, became the norm, and the use of panels and appliqué fell by the way side. New "rules" were attached to the making of medallion quilts during this revival, with the quilts keeping to this coordinated look. An article on medallion quilts in *Quilter's Newsletter Magazine*, June 1982, stated the following:

> "Borders should repeat some element or idea of the central panel, thereby enhancing it. The borders and panel can be related by theme (such as patriotic motifs), by one or more colors in common, or by shapes that are repeated in both." *

* *"Medallion Quilts, Part 1," Quilter's Newsletter Magazine, June 1982, page 7*

If you compare the quilts of the nineteenth century with the quilts of the 1980s, you will see a vast difference in style. Whereas the nineteenth-century quilts were made using whatever was available and obviously working with limited amounts of each fabric, the quilts of the 1980s were based on abundant fabric and fabrics that were designed for the purpose of coordinating all the elements of the centers and borders of these quilts. You also see a difference in the piecing quality. Many of the older medallions had borders that weren't designed to fit perfectly. A lot of their charm is that the borders just ended where they may. Today's quilters have an aversion to this haphazard style of piecing, preferring that everything fit exactly. This makes drafting and a working knowledge of geometry and math very helpful in the creation of medallion quilts.

Whichever style you lean toward, there are still the basics of design and skill involved.

Your quilt can be as modern as you can possibly make it, or a true reproduction of a quilt made by Martha Washington. So let's look at styles in more depth.

Medallion Quilt Styles

When you see various medallion quilts, you might think that some of them contradict our definition above. Often you will see a quilt with a very large center panel and just one elaborate border.

George Washington at Valley Forge, 1976, by Chris Wolf Edmonds

Many Amish quilts can be included in the "center panel" thought process. Whether it is a center of pieced blocks or a center diamond setting, the emphasis on the borders and the elaborate quilting in the outer borders fit the medallion format too well to label the quilt anything else.

Diamond in the Square,
Nine-Patch and Sawtooth variation, by Harriet Hargrave

Comparing the many different quilts that were made in different eras, we want to show that there is a great deal of flexibility and freedom when designing a medallion. Let's look at some of the considerations that might affect your design decisions.

THE CENTER PANEL

The most practical place to start the designing or planning of your medallion quilt is in the center. The center panel will be the focus of the quilt. It establishes the theme and the color scheme; it introduces forms or ideas that might be repeated in the borders; it sets the style for the quilt—whether elegant or whimsical, formal or informal, traditional or contemporary. Your center panel can be made up of any of the following:

❈ A printed panel

❈ Elaborate quilting

❈ A pieced block

❈ Appliqué

❈ Embroidery

Panels were printed in England and used by British quiltmakers as early as 1810, but American quiltmakers did not use them until about 1830. For American quiltmakers, the panels served as a ready source of designs to cut out for Broderie Perse (or chintz appliqué). The British quiltmakers kept the panels intact and usually placed them square in the center of a quilt top, creating the traditional frame format of British quilts. American quilters preferred by far the center medallion format using a large panel in the center surrounded by smaller side panels.*

* Waldvogel, Merikay, "Gallery: Printed Panels for Chintz Quilts: Their Origin and Use," Quilt Index, quiltindex.org/galleryFullRecord.php?kid=5B-B8-1, September 2013

A variety of panels for reproduction quilts

Panels for theme quilts

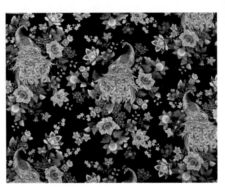

Using yardage to create a panel

Perhaps you have a design for fabulous quilting that never made it to quilt size. Try using it as a center panel to build a quilt around.

Elaborate quilting design by Harriet Hargrave

Appliqué could be the focus of a medallion quilt, continuing the center design into the border, and don't

forget about embroidery. Whether you freehand thread paint like Harriet did to create *Indian Chief* (below) or create a masterpiece from your embroidery machine, what better place to show it off than in the center of a quilt.

Thread-painted *Indian Chief,* embroidered by Harriet Hargrave

Regardless of the method, keep in mind that the center design should be strong enough to merit the border treatment. Strong colors, impressive patterns, or elaborate detail will give your center panel the weight needed to carry the quilt design.

BORDERS

As you can see by comparing the previous photographs, there is no set formula for planning proper proportions for medallion centers and borders. *George Washington at Valley Forge* has relatively little space devoted to borders. Each border is about one-third the width of the center. The single border is the perfect treatment here because it provides a suitable elaborate frame for the center, without overpowering it. This quilt definitely harks back to the original palampores.

Other ideas to make your design more interesting are to use a variety of border widths, to change the color intensity from one border to the next, and to mix techniques. Appliqué, patchwork, and fancy quilting are commonly combined in medallion quilts. When the colors used in the center are also used in the borders, continuity is maintained. *The Virginia Framed Medallion* (page 16) is a perfect example of this.

Repeating shapes or design elements from the center into one or more borders can also create continuity. Symmetry is another way to plan a successful design. Symmetry permits corners to flow and turn.

Here are some questions to ask yourself while designing your quilt:

* ❋ Do you want it to be abstract or representational?
* ❋ Do you want it to be pictorial or geometric?
* ❋ Do you want to showcase a fabric panel or a piece of embroidery?
* ❋ Do you want to celebrate a theme or commemorate an event?
* ❋ Will the quilt be serene or bright?
* ❋ Will the style be casual, formal, elegant, or whimsical?
* ❋ What is the quilt's purpose—a bed quilt or wallhanging?
* ❋ Do you have constraints of size, shape, and details that might affect your design?

FROM THE OUTSIDE IN

There may come a time when you already have some blocks or a particular fabric that you know would look great in a medallion quilt, but know also that it is not right for the center of the quilt. So where do you start? This is the case with *Colorado Memories*.

Colorado Memories, 2010 Shop Hop quilt

The pieced blocks in the large border are the blocks that were provided to us from each of the stores in the 2010 Denver metro area Shop Hop. Not wanting to make a standard block quilt, Carrie turned to Jinny Beyer's medallion book and started thumbing through it. A quilt named *Shenandoah* by Lena Behme was the inspiration for the design of the Shop Hop quilt.

Having an even number of blocks made it a challenge to come up with a medallion setting until Carrie saw the inspiration quilt. Setting the blocks side by side in the corner made it possible to successfully use all twelve blocks and create a very interesting quilt. Because the blocks and the toile fabric were the focus, this quilt was literally designed from the block border in, making it necessary for the pieced center design to fit the space made available by the borders. This is just as much of a challenge as, if not more than, creating your quilt from the center out, but can lead to some great innovation and ingenious ideas to use up space. We will cover this quilt and the thought process more in Class 560.

WALL QUILTS

Wall quilts can cover the gamut in sizes—from a small quilt for a small entryway of your home to one for the atrium of a large office building. Generally, we think of wall quilts as something small for our homes. If you are thinking of making a small medallion quilt, keep in mind that the center panel needs to be small enough to allow room for enough borders to be aesthetically appealing to complete the quilt. Unlike a bed quilt, a wall quilt does not necessarily need to fit a predetermined size. Its size is somewhat flexible, which makes the planning easier.

A wall quilt's shape is also flexible. You can make the quilt square, rectangular, round, or even octagonal. The center panel can be the shape of the quilt with even borders on all sides, or you can start with one shape and end up with another by adding a unique arrangement of borders.

BED QUILTS

Unlike a wall quilt, the complete surface of a bed quilt is not seen at the same time. Instead, distinct design areas are separated by the shape of the bed: the drop at the foot and the sides of the bed, the top mattress surface, as well as the pillow area. Many antique quilts are made of symmetrical borders around the center regardless of the size and dimensions of the bed. You might find that you prefer to design your quilt to fit specific spaces. If you are concerned that the quilt be pleasing to see at any angle, you might want to work with shapes, colors, or themes that are in common, helping make the quilt work as a total unit. A medallion quilt for a bed should be planned carefully if it is to have graceful, coherent borders and still fit the bed as intended. We will discuss later working out the design on graph paper to get a feel for how well the elements work together.

DESIGNING BORDERS

Traditional medallion quilts generally have random borders of various sizes added to the center panel or block. Many of the quilts look as if the borders were well thought out and planned; others are a variety of leftover scraps and colors that have no relationship to one another. Medallion quilts made in the 1980s and 1990s appear more planned and fabricated. Fabrics are used repeatedly, elements of the center block are repeated in the borders, and so on. Jinny Beyer's medallion quilts are examples of this. The possibilities are endless when it comes to the design of the borders for the quilt. By studying the many quilts of each era, you have endless ideas to consider in this phase of the quilt.

Blue Star Sapphire, 1982, 88" × 95", by Jinny Beyer

One of the easiest ways to make a decorative border fit the preceding border or center panel is to use appliqué. Either the border or the center panel (or both) can be done in appliqué. If the center is pieced and the border is appliquéd, you simply make the border strips whatever length is required to fit the pieced panel. Choose the border width to suit your appliqué motif. Since the background size for a given appliqué design is so flexible, it is easy to make an appliqué border fit any dimension required. You can even adjust the number of leaves in a traditional motif or alter the position of a flower to fit the background area perfectly. The appliqué can be fluid and free flowing, or designed specifically to fit the space.

If the center panel is appliquéd and the first border is pieced, make the background of the center a little larger than needed, piece the inner borders, and trim the center to fit the borders. You can also plan all this on graph paper first and make the center fit the borders.

Another easy way to make borders fit is to make the borders from blocks related in size to the blocks in the center panel. Even if the center panel is rectangular, the border will fit if you use this technique.

If the border is made from blocks set straight and the center panel is made from blocks set diagonally, the border block dimensions should be related to the *diagonal* measurement of the center block. Another way to design border blocks that have related dimensions is to use *part* of the center block as the border block. Using elements or partial blocks is a way to create cohesion of all the elements throughout the entire quilt. This process not only makes a naturally fitting border, but it also saves measuring and figuring.

You can also design pieced borders by regrouping shapes introduced in the center panel. Borders designed from shapes in the center panel look natural, but they may require some careful planning.

When planning pieced borders, it is often necessary to add a plain border between the outer pieced border and the center pieced or appliquéd portion of the quilt. This also works between two pieced borders when the math does not work out evenly. You can make any two parts fit each other by adding a strip of just the right width between them. To determine the strip width needed, you can piece the inner border and then piece the outer border, which is longer. Measure the lengths of the two top borders and subtract to find the difference in lengths. Divide the difference by 2. This tells you the width the plain border needs to be on each side of the quilt. Measure the inner and outer side borders, and divide the difference by 2 to find the width of the plain top and bottom borders.

Example: If the outer top border measures 50″ and the inner border measures 42″, the difference is 8″. Dividing 8″ by 2, you get a width of 4″ needed for the plain side borders. The outer and inner pieced and appliquéd side borders measure 67″ and 59″, respectively. The difference is 8″, so the plain borders at top and bottom would be 4″ wide. It is important here to note, and we will talk about it later in this chapter as well as in the quilt chapters, that on rectangular quilts these filler borders may not always measure the same on the top and bottom as they do on the sides in order to make your chosen block size work. This is okay and a practice regularly seen in all medallions.

As you can see, careful planning and measuring are necessary to get these quilts to fit together properly. Besides planning borders, you can work with either square or rectangular quilts. Obviously, square quilts have an advantage over rectangular ones.

SQUARE QUILTS

Symmetry is a key element to successful border designs that incorporate natural corners. When pieced or appliquéd borders end at the same point in the design on each side of the quilt, it is easy to work out a successful corner treatment. Because of this, it is easier to design a square medallion quilt than a rectangular one. For a square quilt, you can plan the border and corner for just one side and simply repeat them on the other three sides. By centering the border on each side, and by reversing any directional patterns at the border centers, you can be assured that the borders will be symmetrical and the corners will match.

A square quilt can simplify border planning. The quilt *Geese in Flight* (below) is a good example. The center block is square. On either side of the center block are dogtooth triangles. These repeating triangles are made a particular size, determined by dividing the size of the center block by the desired size of the triangles. If the desired size does not come out even, change the size of the triangles until they fit as desired. Because the center block is square, all the borders are the same.

Geese in Flight, 2014, by Harriet Hargrave

As borders are added, the calculations are similar. Once you have designed the pieced border, the addition of plain strips between the center block and the pieced border helps with the fitting.

Square quilts make great wall hangings, and they fit queen- and king-size beds well. It is also easy to come up with a square center panel or block, matching corners and borders that are even all around the quilt.

RECTANGULAR QUILTS

What if you have a need for a rectangular quilt? How do you plan borders to fit a rectangular quilt? If you are making the quilt to fit a particular bed, you probably want the borders to drop at the sides and bottom of the bed to match. It is generally easiest to turn the center block or panel into a rectangle, but there are other solutions:

❋ Set a square block on point and add large corner triangles that can be trimmed to a rectangle.

❋ Add an extra top and bottom border to extend the length of the quilt.

Once the center is turned into a rectangle, the subsequent pieced borders can be even all around, but they will have to fit two different measurements for length and width. Since the best way to round a corner gracefully is to have borders ending symmetrically on either side of the corner, you should plan your pieced border motifs to end at the same point in the design in lengthwise and crosswise borders. You can achieve this by adjusting the width of plain strips between pieced borders, or you can adjust the size of the border patches *slightly* for a perfect fit. A better solution is to make the border from units that repeat at a certain distance relative to the previous border pattern. The illustration (below right) shows the outer pieced border made from units that repeat in a space equal to the diagonal measurement of the blocks in the previous border. The points line up naturally, and the borders end symmetrically for matching corners.

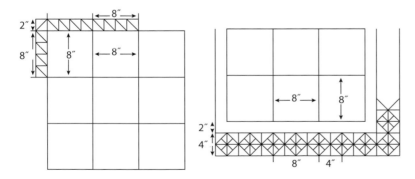

A solution found in many antique quilts is to place spacers in various positions to make up for size deviations in the border. This problem occurred in the construction of *The Virginia Framed Medallion*. Spacers were needed at the ends of the Ohio Star borders to keep the math ruler-friendly for the star blocks.

Detail of corner where spacers were added to
The Virginia Framed Medallion

DESIGNING WITH GRAPH PAPER

There are a number of ways to approach designing a medallion quilt on graph paper. Perhaps the easiest way is to start by drawing a single block. This is the case with the incorporated-border medallion quilt *Peppermint Delight* (page 59). This quilt idea all started with a quilt Carrie caught a glimpse of in one of Harriet's many books, but could never find again. So working from memory and out of *Quilter's Academy Vol. 2* and *Vol. 3*, she worked with incorporated-border blocks and just repeated them to create "borders" within the quilt. In some regards, this is the easiest medallion quilt to make. You are still making an all-block quilt with a diagonal setting. Pieced border blocks of different designs but of the same size are used rather than trying to make different borders fit as you grow your quilt.

Drawing of a single block
repeated to create a border

Drawing of *Peppermint Delight*

This repeated-block type of medallion quilt can also be seen in Harriet's *Softly Spoken* medallion (page 77), but with a special center and some plain borders added to show off beautiful quilting.

The majority of medallion quilts you might want to design will probably be more traditional, having a center panel and many different borders surrounding it.

It is here that we cannot stress enough the need to have a lot of inspiration photos to help you out, as well as Class 590 (page 98) of this book. As you look through our library of borders in Class 590, you may come across one or several that you like the looks of and would like to make. You may see a photo of a quilt on the Internet that feels good overall. Study the quilt and determine what borders are used to create the quilt and if all of them appeal to you, or just a few. Once you have some source material it is time to go shopping, either in your stash at home or in your local quilt shop. See if you can find a fabric that would work for your center panel, or as mentioned earlier, make or use something you already have appliquéd or embroidered. If that center panel is already a given size, you know where you are going to start on your graph paper. Begin by drawing that size in the exact center of your paper. The next question, which may seem like getting the cart before the horse, is to ask yourself, what size do you want this quilt to finish? Do you want it for a wall, a throw on the sofa, a lap quilt for a loved one, or a bed quilt? Draw that square or rectangle on the graph paper so you know how much space you need to fill.

Softly Spoken, 2014, by Harriet Hargrave

These types of quilts may start from being inspired by a fabric or fabric line that you want to showcase as a cohesive group, not having one fabric be the star of the show in the center and the others be supporting players. This is also a great type of medallion to make in two colors or in shades and hues of a single color. Once you have your blocks drawn out, you may want to play with coloration with your colored pencils. Make photocopies of your original line drawing, fill in the colors differently, and see what happens.

Peppermint Delight with color variations

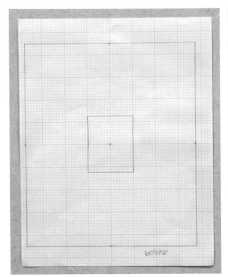

Drawing of center panel and planned
finished size of quilt

After that, it is filling in the blanks.
Depending on how busy or subdued
your center is, you need to decide if
you want to start with a plain border
or a pieced one. Now you are off and
running. If you choose to start with
a plain border, what size does it need
to be? You really don't know until
you have chosen the next border you
want, probably a pieced border. So
choose the pieced border you want,
and draft it to fit the size and shape
of your center.

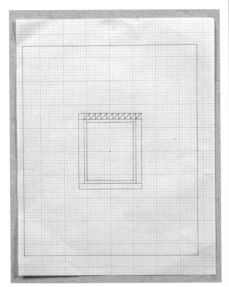

Center panel drawn and a pieced
border starting to be drawn at a
certain distance from center panel

tip Keep in mind you may end
up working in ⅛" units a
lot to make these borders fit. So long
as it is a number that you can find on
your ruler you can likely make your
blocks fit that size. It is also helpful to
note that prime numbers (numbers
only divisible by themselves and 1)
sometimes occur in your quilt as
you are drafting it. These measurements are something that you can
avoid having in your quilt by simply
manipulating a plain border. Here is a
list of prime numbers up to 101:
3, 5, 7, 11, 13, 17, 19, 23, 29, 31, 37, 41, 43,
47, 53, 59, 61, 67, 71, 73, 79, 83, 89, 97, 101

As was discussed earlier, you may find
yourself designing from the outside
in. Let's say you find a border in the
library of borders in Class 590 that
you think would look great for the
final border of the bed quilt you want
to design. So draw that border the size
that will fit your estimated quilt size
and work in, maybe placing a plain
border as the next border in, and so
on. If you know the size and shape
of your center and the size and shape
you want your finished quilt, it then
just becomes a matter of filling space
in as simple or complicated a way as
you wish or as your skills will allow.

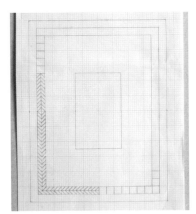

Center panel drawn and a pieced
border starting to be drawn
around the outside edge

You will start to find that the plain
borders are your friends and can help
make your chosen pieced borders
work out simply by manipulating
their width. Earlier we talked about
these borders being a different size.
The side borders may need to be narrower and the top and bottom wider
in order to keep your math friendly
for your next pieced border. It should
be noted here, too, that when you
are actually piecing these quilts it is
always a good idea to cut these borders at least ½" wider than you think
they should be just in case your quilt
is smaller or larger or your next border
is smaller or larger than planned. You
can use the width of the plain border
to keep you on track with your plan.

As we mentioned earlier, especially
when you are working with a
rectangular quilt, you may find that
in order to make things work you will
need to make your blocks a slightly
different size or your plain borders a
little different size to make everything
fit. Cornerstones that can be repeated
as a design element can come in
handy to help you make those
transitions easier.

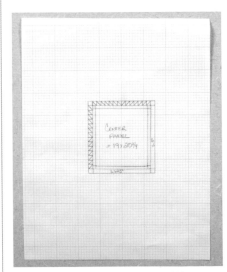

Drawing of a border with two different-
sized blocks with a repeating rectangular
cornerstone to make everything fit

We really do wish there was a magic formula we could give you or a wand we could wave that would make this all work and be clear, but unfortunately it all comes with trial and error and in the doing of it. There are so many designs out there and so many different styles that there is no one way to teach designing and drafting. You may decide that designing your own is just too much work. Harriet is challenged by figuring out the sizes and dimensions of what she sees when working with old quilts and inspiring photos of old quilts. Carrie instinctively heads for graph paper and colored pencils, and the ideas just start to flow. Her own innate need to be original and creative takes over. Both approaches bring you back to the fact that medallion quilts take a lot of calculator work and planning. The reason we saved these quilts for your master's study is that it takes a full toolbox of skills to do the piecing. If you have these skills, you can put all your energy into design and drafting.

It also needs to be discussed here that your quilt may take on a life of its own. You may have everything drawn out perfectly on paper, colored in how you think it will look nicest, but as you start creating borders your quilt starts talking to you, and when you put the next border up, the quilt may say, "That doesn't look so good on me." Listen to that—don't just plow ahead just because you had a plan on paper. Sit down with your inspiration photo or border library again and reevaluate.

This happened with Carrie's *Fancy Tail Feathers*. When she got to the final outer border, the half-square triangles she had planned and the color layout she wanted were just too heavy and stark for the outer border she was using. By playing with the elements she had, she turned the half-square triangles into quarter-square triangles, made the plain border right next to the outer border a little different size, and now is much happier with the outcome of the quilt. This is the quilt talking back to you.

Fancy Tail Feathers finished

You can design your quilt solely by the seat of your pants too! Pick a center, and then pick a border. You may need to draft out each border to be sure the blocks will fit the size of the quilt, but it will save you from tons of drafting of the blocks over and over. Then add a plain border and then another pieced border—let your quilt just talk to you. These quilts are labors of love and may take weeks or months to create. Maybe you only add a single border every other week. If in the end you have a masterpiece that you love, what does it matter how long it took to create! Have fun with this. Don't let the thoughts of the math and drafting bog you down; this really isn't an intimidating process, especially if you have worked with us through the first four volumes of *Quilter's Academy*.

> *note* It is here we want to address something important. If you do choose to reproduce a quilt you find on the Internet and you plan to hang that quilt in a show or for any reason ever publish your quilt on the Internet or in a book, we ask that you make sure you give full credit to the person whose quilt it was that inspired you. Anything older than 84 years no longer has a copyright, but if a person or a museum owns the quilt, you need to give credit to that person or entity of ownership. Being inspired by someone's work is actually the highest form of praise for that person. By acknowledging them, your work will shine because you are giving credit where credit is due. This is important to your integrity as a quilter as well as the integrity of the original work and its maker.

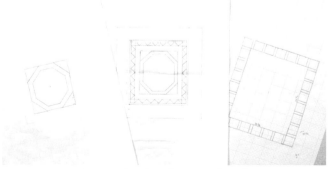
Preliminary drawing of *Fancy Tail Feathers*

Class 530

Medallion quilts can be made by any quilter as long as you pick borders that are appropriate to your current skill level. The first two quilts in this book are geared specifically to the new and beginning quilter. If you haven't mastered all the skills throughout *Quilter's Academy Vols. 1–4*, you should still be able to make these two quilts. Both were inspired by quilts Carrie found on the Internet after a very long image search for simple medallions.

> *note* We want to emphasize here before you start the importance of having your seam allowance set so that you have accurate "finished" units, not a perfect seam allowance. If the measurement from seam to seam of a finished unit is not the exact measurement, none of the quilts in this book are going to fit together properly, if at all, as they get more complicated. Please take the time to get your seam allowance and your ironing skills perfected before attempting any of the medallions in the book.

When beginning this process, Carrie wanted to make a very unintimidating quilt, a medallion that anyone could make. Because of the current popularity of charm squares, she chose to work with the 5″ size of the squares. This is a nice place to begin with drafting as you literally are just drawing out squares. No triangles, no diamonds, no stars, just squares and borders. By using a precut piece of fabric you already know what size some of your borders will be, thereby making it easier to figure out what size the "plain" borders need to be. This quilt, because of its simplicity, becomes a great platform to really show off the quilting. The colors were great, but the quilting was far more exciting and the large open expanses of the border beckon for fun quilting.

The aim of the second quilt was to keep the borders fairly simple and easily pieced. There are very few triangles, making this a quilt that can be made by someone who has worked through *Quilter's Academy Vol. 1* and is ready for a slightly bigger challenge. Carrie's inspiration for this quilt was found during an Internet search that led her to a photo of a quilt made by a lady in Australia.

The inspiration quilt had a very busy and interesting fabric cut into a circle in the center surrounded by triangles, which is what caught Carrie's eye. From there, while using the borders of the inspiration quilt as a guide, Carrie's quilt varies greatly in the overall feel and look, because she changed the scale and placement of the borders and added a couple from our border design chapter.

Designing your own medallion can be that easy and as you will see a little further on, in Class 550 (Carrie's *Fancy Tail Feather* quilt), you can make very elegant medallions with fairly simple blocks. We hope you enjoy this journey as much as we have in finding and making these quilts to share with you!

All About the Quilting

Quilt top size: 48″ × 48″

As mentioned, with the popularity of charm squares and charm packs, this quilt is a very easy one to plan. Find a color palette or collection of fabrics you love and a background that complements them, and you are ready to make your first medallion quilt top.

Basics of Design

We are going to start this quilt at the beginning. To learn the design aspects of these quilts, and this quilt in particular, you will need basic graph paper (four-to-the-inch or eight-to-the-inch), a pencil, an eraser, and some colored pencils. Find the center of your paper. From the exact center of the paper, count outward horizontally and vertically 4½ squares, and make a mark.

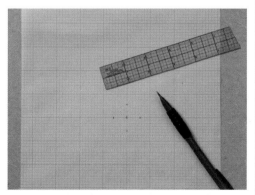

Drawing of 4 dots at 4½ squares each from centerlines on your graph paper

Connect the dots so you have a box in the center of your paper.

Connecting the 4 dots

> note   *Remember that when drafting a quilt you are always going to work with finished measurements, not cut sizes.*

Count from the lines you just drew out another 4½ squares on all four sides and connect the marks corner to corner. To represent the seams between the different-colored squares, draw a line right on the centerline, then another line 4½ squares above it and another line 4½ squares below it. Do the same on all four sides of your quilt drawing.

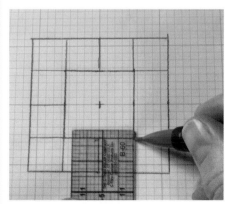

Drawing the first border and adding in seamlines

Next draw a box around this one, 4½ squares away again. This represents the next border, which is solid. It is advised that you draw in the seamlines at the corners for these solid borders. This will help you to start thinking about how you are going to construct the quilt as well as help you figure yardage when the time comes. We recommend that you sew the side borders on first and then add the top and bottom borders. You will need a seamline drawn to show this.

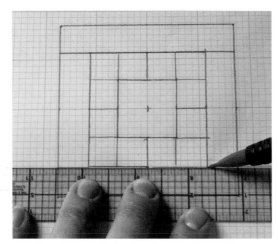
Drawing of solid border drawn with seamlines

Draw your third border next. This is a pieced border, so draw in the seamlines every 4½ squares above, below, and to either side of the centerline.

Drawing of third border with seamlines for squares

Finally, draw in your final outer solid border. Make a box around the last border and connect the lines in the corners. Add the appropriate seamlines.

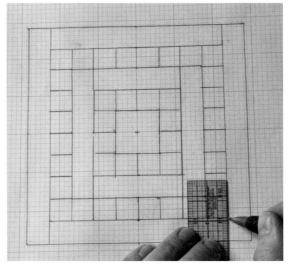
Complete quilt drawn out

And there you have it; you have drafted your first medallion. We wish we could say that they will all be this simple.

Yardage:

40 – 5″ squares or an assortment of fat quarters (as many or few as you choose, but no less than 8 different fabrics) for colored borders

1¼–1⅜ yards of coordinating fabric*

The difference in the yardage needed will depend on what type of fabric you choose for your "solid" border. If you are using a solid or other fabric where a diagonal spliced seam will show and not look good, you may choose to purchase the larger quantity of fabric and work with lengthwise-grain borders. This yardage also reflects cutting your solid borders exactly to width, which may be okay in this quilt but in future quilts you will definitely want to add ½″–1″ more than what you think the cut border needs to be, just in case you need to use that width to do some measurement adjusting for the next border of the quilt.

Construction

Start by cutting your center square. If you are working with squares that are 5″ cut, 4½″ finished, you will need to cut a 9½″ square to start your medallion.

BORDER 1

Sew two sets of 2 – 5″ squares together, and iron and trim them to exact measurements as we have taught throughout this series. Add these two sets onto opposite sides of the center square. Next, sew together four squares, iron and trim, and add them to the top and bottom of the center square, aligning your seam allowances as needed.

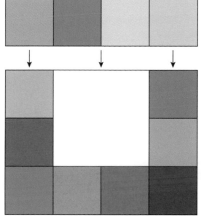

Center square with a set of side
squares attached and another set
ready to be attached

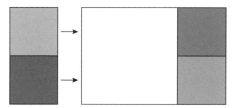

Center square with bottom squares attached
and top set ready to be attached

BORDER 2

This is the first plain border, and whether you are working with lengthwise grain or across the width of the fabric, you will need:

❈ 2 – 18½″* strips 5″ wide*, for sides

❈ 2 – 27½″* strips 5″ wide, for top and bottom

Be sure to measure your quilt top through the middle and in a couple of other locations to be sure it is straight and square.

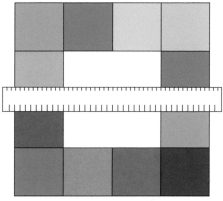

Ruler on top of quilt top
(center square and first border attached)

Draw a line at the actual length needed on each end of the borders, measure ½″ beyond the length, and draw a line. This allows you to square the corners once the borders are added. If needed, refer back to *Volume 1*, Class 180 (page 97). This is something you will want to make a habit of to keep the corners square.

> *note* Use your best judgment at this point if you think you need to cut these borders a little wider or not. Most likely not, as you are only crossing a very few seam allowances, but if you want to start getting yourself in the habit of making your plain borders a little wider and then trimming then down, this is a good place to start. Borders are no different than sewing strip sets and the accuracy of trimming continually pays off big dividends in keeping every finished unit accurate. Every time you cross over a seam, a tiny bit of width is eaten up. By cutting wider and trimming, the border can be trimmed to be the exact measurement needed. If your quilt at this point isn't the width/length it should be based on your measurements from your graph paper drawing, this is where you can adjust by cutting this plain border a little wider or narrower depending on your quilt top's needs. The addition of ¼″ to ½″ is recommended.

Sew these borders onto your quilt. Your quilt top should now measure 27½" with seam allowances.

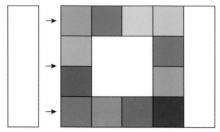

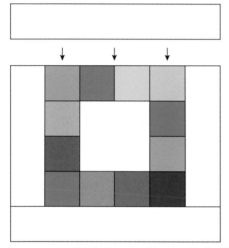

Center square with a set of side borders attached and another set ready to be attached

Center square with bottom border attached and top set ready to be attached

BORDER 3

This again is a pieced border using your 5" squares. For the two sides, sew 6 squares together, ironing and trimming in between each addition. Sew 8 squares together for the top and bottom. Attach the sides first and then the top and bottom. Your quilt top should now measure 36½".

BORDER 4

This is the final border. Cut 2 – 36½" and 2 – 45½" borders 5" wide or wider. See tip.

> **tip** Because Harriet and Carrie quilt their own quilts, they prefer to leave about 2" extra on the outside edge of the final border. This extension works as a "handle" so that there is something to hold onto while quilting the final border at the edge. It also allows for trimming a perfect-width border after the quilting is completed, measuring from the seam to the desired finished width plus seam allowance for binding.

That's it! You have successfully, and we hope quickly, created your very first medallion quilt. Have fun picking the quilting designs for this project. Quilting is what the borders of this quilt are all about.

Summer Market

Quilt top size: 60″ × 60″

Basics of Design

As was mentioned earlier, Carrie found a quilt on the Internet that inspired this quilt. A printed pear stripe fabric added to the excitement. Carrie felt this fabric had to be added to the design, making her quilt instantly very different from the inspiration quilt. An inspiration quilt is really only a starting point. Harriet is inspired to delve into her stash to find a fabric that mimics a fabric in the original quilt she is reproducing. For Carrie, a touchstone is needed to start her brain into a series of "what if" questions.

Original drawing of quilt

Those "what if" questions play a big role in starting to design a medallion. In Carrie's case, the pears were not large enough to make a good outer border, so they needed to somehow be incorporated into the center part of the medallion. With this quilt being a "starter" medallion, she wanted to keep the math aspect of the design as simple as possible. The pears of the border fabric she chose measured 2¾″ finished. That made the math a little messy, but not too bad. It just meant that this quilt had to be built partly from the inside out, but also from the outside in.

Starting with a 12″ center was the easy decision. As the appliquéd center circle could be made any size, the surrounding block measurement was more important. Determining the size of the half-square triangles was next, so Carrie referred back to the inspiration quilt. These blocks are large on the original quilt, so Carrie made hers equal in proportion to her center, making this border 3″ finished.

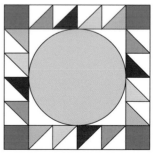

Drawing of center square and first border

Still wanting to maintain the flavor of the inspiration quilt, Carrie determined that the next border size (a plain border) should be 1″ finished.

This is where the interesting math comes in. The pears are a fairly small in scale and are likely to get lost if they were put as the border beyond the nine-patches. If Carrie continued to follow her inspiration quilt, the pears needed to be closer to the center, as one of the next two borders. Because the pears measure 2¾″, the border next to the pears would need to be 1¼″, 2¼″, or 3¼″ to keep the math ruler-friendly. When playing around on several sheets of graph paper with the pears and those size borders drawn to scale, she determined that the 2¼″ size looked the best with the pears.

The next question was, what sort of pieced border can you make that will look nice at 2¼″? That measurement is really only divisible by 2 or 3 in order to result in ruler- and quilter-friendly measurements. Four-patches and nine-patches are options, but *Ah-ha!* Rail blocks! They are in the inspiration quilt, but in a different location, so why not use them? They also keep this quilt easier to make. So, 2¼″ Rail blocks were drawn in, and then the solid border that would be cut from the pear fabric.

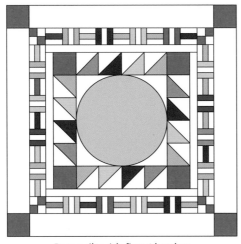

Pear quilt with first 4 borders

A tiny math issue cropped up using a 2¼″ border. It doesn't end in a nice round number of blocks for the size the quilt is currently. The quilt top after the second border is added measures 20″ square. 20″ ÷ 2¼″ = 8.8888, not a ruler-friendly measurement. So, what is the solution? Taking a page out of the book of the old-time quilters, just chop this off! If you sew nine 2¼″ blocks together, you get 20¼″ + ½″ for seam allowance. So, Carrie centered a long ruler with the blocks, measured from the center out 10¼″, and cut off the extra bit. Then with the addition of 4 four-patch blocks in the corners, problem solved, border made, and once the pear border is sewn on, the quilt is back to being easy math again. Are you starting to see why these quilts are fun to make?

The quilt according to the graph paper drawing is now 30″ square. There are a lot of block sizes that divide evenly into 30″: 1″, 1¼″, 1½″, 2″, 2½″, and so on. Back to the inspiration quilt again: nine-patches—big nine-patches. To make the colors alternate, you need an odd number of blocks. As for the math, 30 ÷ 7 is not a nice number, 30″ ÷ 5 = 6″, and 30″ ÷ 3 = 10″; 10″ is entirely too big for the blocks, so 6″ blocks it is. Each square within a 6″ nine-patch is 2″. We love nice math! This border gets drawn on now that you have found the size needed.

Quilt with nine-patch borders added

The quilt is getting bigger and it's looking like it is time for another plain border. Something simple to keep your attention on the fun colors of the pieced borders and the pears. Let's have it mimic the pear border, but in a friendly size, 3″ instead of 2¾″. Once that decision is made, you can add a 3″ solid border.

In looking at the inspiration quilt for the last time, Carrie found there is another pieced border for the outer border. So, that decision is made too: one more pieced border. But what should it be? Flipping through the index of borders we had assembled (Class 590, page 98), Carrie found a variation on Amish Shadows and the *Confetti* quilt she made in *Volume 2* (page 77) of the series. What size should this be? The quilt at this point is measuring 48″ square, again a number that many other numbers divide nicely into. Now we are dealing with diagonally set units. What sizes of diagonal squares will divide evenly into 48″? Carrie started with the obvious, 6″ × 8 = 48″; furthermore, 6″ ÷ 1.414 = 4¼″. Great, that makes life easy. The white squares in the center will be 4¼″ finished, and the strip-pieced side-setting triangles need to have a long measurement of 6″ finished. Now these borders can be added to your drawing.

Pears

Final layout of *Summer Market*

Once you have your drawing, calculate the yardage needed for the fabrics you are using. Below is a list of the yardages used for Carrie's quilt.

Harriet's Note

These instructions have been written this way so that you can change any of the borders to fit the fabric you have chosen. By breaking down how Carrie made her decisions, you can work through the same process using different fabrics and sizes. This is the beginning of the purpose of this book. It is what makes designing and constructing medallion quilts so much fun. All the decisions are yours to make.

Yardage:

16 or more fat quarters; Carrie used 24 different colors.

2⅛ yards minimum, at least ½ yard more if you are using a very large variety of fat quarters and will be doing a lot of short piecing

1 yard second, complementary background for center square and border 6

1 yard* fabric for focus fabric borders (pears in this case)

* More if your fabric does not have even repeats or you have to fussy cut the borders from your chosen fabric.

Construction

This quilt starts out with a center block that has a circle appliquéd onto it. Perhaps you have or can find a fabric that already has a circle motif to it that you can just cut out and appliqué down. Or you can create your own circle motif with elements from a fabric you plan to use in the quilt.

The pears are buttonhole stitched onto a background fabric (the green) that was then cut into a 12″ circle and appliquéd to the background square using Harriet's invisible machine appliqué technique. In Harriet's book *Mastering Machine Appliqué*, the buttonhole stitch appliqué method is covered (Blanket Stitch Appliqué Techniques, page 62); the invisible machine appliqué technique is also covered thoroughly (Invisible Machine Applique Techniques, page 88).

The fabric for the circle was cut into a 12″-diameter circle. The edges are turned over freezer paper (¼″ seam allowance) and appliquéd to the background, making the circle finish at 11½″. Because the appliqué process can cause the background square of fabric to contract a little, the actual square of fabric the circle was appliquéd to was cut 13½″. After the circle was attached, it was squared and cut down to 12½″.

BORDER 1

This border is composed of 16 half-square triangles and 4 cornerstones. Each of these elements measures 3″ finished.

To make the half-square triangles, refer back to *Quilter's Academy Vol. 3*, Lesson Three (page 12) and pick your favorite method. The Sew and Slice—Method #2 was used here since only 4 each of 4 different colors of triangles were needed. Cut 8 – 4″ squares of background fabric and 2 – 4″ squares of each of the 4 colors you are using. The cornerstones are cut 3½″ and added to the ends of the top and bottom segments of this border.

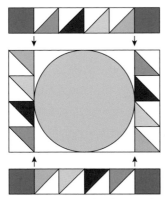

Center square with side triangle borders attached, ready to add top and bottom borders

Once these borders are sewn on, measure your quilt top. It should measure 18½″ square.

BORDER 2

The first of just three plain borders is next. This border will be 1″ wide finished, 1½″ cut, or as we discussed earlier you may want to cut the border a little bit wider to compensate for any contraction that may happen or seam allowances it will go over.

You will need to cut 2 – 18½″ borders and 2 – 20½″ borders whatever width (1½″ or wider) you deem you need. Add the sides first, then the top and bottom borders.

Once this border is on, square the corners, and trim if necessary to make sure the border is exactly 1¼″ wide. Your quilt top should now measure 20½″.

BORDER 3

This small rail and post border is easy to create. If you need a refresher, refer back to *Quilter's Academy Vol. 1*, Lesson Seven (page 33). Carrie chose to use 9 different fabrics and created the 36 rails and posts needed by cutting 4 – 1¼″-wide fabric strips and subcutting 9 – 12″-long strips. She also cut a 1¼″ strip from each of the 9 colored fabrics and then cut off a 12″-long strip. Sew these 2 strips together, iron and trim, and then cut the strips in half so you now have 18 – 6″ strips. To 10 of these strips, add another 6″ strip of the background. To the other 8 you will add a 6″ strip of the same color. You should be able to cut these strip sets, once sewn, into 20 – 2¾″ segments of background-color-background and 16 – 2¾″ segments of color-background-color.

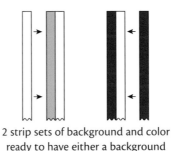

2 strip sets of background and color ready to have either a background or another color strip added

6″ strip sets cut into 2 – 2¾″ segments with little waste

Lay out nine of the segments you just created, alternating from a light-dark-light segment that will be oriented horizontally to a dark-light-dark segment that will be vertical. You will end up with a light-dark-light segment at the end of each of the 4 borders you are creating.

Layout of the rail and post border

Once you have these borders sewn together you will need to trim them down to fit the length of your quilt top. Find the center of your rail and post border and position your ruler with the 10¼″ line on that center mark. Be sure to align the seams with the ruler lines, and then cut off any excess of the last post block. Flip the border around and do the same on the other end.

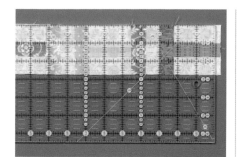

The rail and post border to size

To create the 4 four-patch blocks for the cornerstones you will need a 14″ strip each of a color and your background. Sew these together, iron and trim, and then subcut them into 8 – 1⅝″ segments. Flip half of these segments around and create the four-patches. For a refresher, refer back to *Quilter's Academy Vol. 1*, Lesson Six (page 57). Add these four-patches to the end of 2 of the freshly trimmed rail and post borders.

Sew the two side borders on first and then add the top and bottom borders, making sure you align any seams as necessary.

Adding rail and post borders to quilt

Measure your quilt top. It should measure 25″ square.

BORDER 4

Carrie chose this to be her pear border, which required a little special handling. On the printed fabric she had to find the center of the pears, line a ruler up with that center, and cut her border 3¼″ wide. The side borders need to measure 25″, and the top and bottom borders need to measure 31″. Once the strips were cut with the pears centered, the border could be cut to length with the pears centered with the quilt center.

BORDER 5

This is the nine-patch border. For this border, Carrie chose a very scrappy look and used 12 different fabrics for 24 blocks. There is a block with 5 dark squares and a block with 4 dark squares of each different fabric.

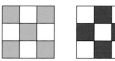

Two different color layouts of nine-patches

The math for figuring the amount of fabric needed is now easy. You need 3 segments of light-dark-light and three segments of dark-light-dark—resulting in 3 – 8″-long strips, 2½″ wide, of each of the colors and 7 full strips (width of fabric) of the background, subcut into 36 – 8″ lengths. For a reminder on making nine-patches refer back to *Quilter's Academy Vol. 1*, Lesson Three (page 74).

For the two side borders, you will need to start and end your rows with one of the nine-patch blocks with only 4 colored squares.

Side border configuration

For the top and bottom borders you will start and end with the nine-patches with 5 colored squares.

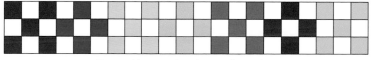

Top and bottom border configuration

Add these borders to your quilt, and now your quilt top should measure 42½″ square.

BORDER 6

Border 6 is another solid border. Our quilt uses the same fabric as the background of the center square for flow and consistency.

These borders are cut 3½" wide or wider if you want to trim them down after attaching them to the nine-patch border, which is recommended, as you are sewing over a number of seam allowances that could make the border a little wobbly on the edge.

You will need 2 strips 42½" long plus ½" on each end for fudge factor, and 2 – 48½"-long strips. These will need to be spliced together to create the needed length for this border. These borders could also be cut with the lengthwise grain, if you purchased enough fabric to do this. Again, add side borders first, then top and bottom. Square up your corners and trim if necessary.

Now you are ready to tackle the final border.

BORDER 7

This is a very fun border to create. We talked a little about creating pieced side-setting triangles in *Quilter's Academy Vol. 2*, Lesson Three (pages 98–100). This is the same idea. We will start with making the striped triangles.

You will be sewing together three strips: a color, a background, and another color.

In order to make the strips exactly 1" finished, the two colored strips need to be cut 1¾". These will get sewn to either side of a background strip that is cut 1½".

If you are using fat quarters for this quilt and have a large variety of colors, this is a good place to have fun mixing and matching your colors.

When you are sewing the strips together, keep in mind you can get a side-setting triangle from a 7"-long strip set and 2 triangles with opposite color placement from a 12" strip set. You need 64 side-setting triangles, so plan your segment lengths accordingly.

Once your strip sets are created, you need to cut them. Using a 90° triangle ruler, position the lines that run across the ruler exactly on the seamlines of your strip sets. Have the point of the ruler exactly on the top edge and keep the lines and seams straight with each other. You will be alternating the ruler back and forth to get two colorways from each strip.

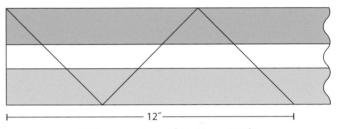

Cutting strips into side-setting triangles

Once you have all 64 of your side-setting triangles cut, you will need to cut the 36 squares. These squares will finish at 4¼", making them 4¾" cut. You will need 4 strips* of background fabric.

Note: You may actually need or want to cut 5 strips. If your fabric is not a full 44" wide you will not get the 9 squares out of each strip and may need a couple of extras. This extra strip was calculated into the yardage above.

Sew two side-setting triangles to opposite sides of one of your squares as shown in the following illustration.

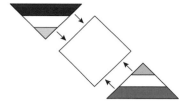

Attaching side-setting triangles to squares

Position two squares at each end of each border that will only have a single side-setting triangle attached to each. See the illustration.

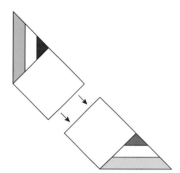

Two end square/triangle sets for border

Do not attach these to the ends of your borders; instead attach them to each other by sewing the squares together. This will create the corners and will save you from having to sew a mitered seam at the end of each border. To attach the long borders to your quilt top, align the triangles with the edge of the quilt, with ⅜″ of the triangle tip hanging over the end of your quilt top, and pin the whole border in place to ensure you also have ⅜″ of a tail overhanging on the opposite end as well.

Sew the side borders on first and then the top and bottom borders. To position the points at the ends of the borders, draw the ¼″ seam allowance onto the wrong side of the triangle points as well as on the corners of the plain

borders you are attaching them to. Put a pin at the intersection of each corner and pin them together. Sew off the end of each triangle as you attach each border. Do this carefully, as the next step will need the angle of these triangles to be true to keep the corner square. If you need a refresher on how to add borders in this fashion, refer to *Quilter's Academy Vol. 1*, Class 180, Lesson Four (pages 98 and 99) for applying mitered borders as that technique and this are the same.

Once you have all the borders attached, it is time to add the corner pieces you created earlier. Align the seam allowances as shown in the illustration, pin the piece in place, and sew.

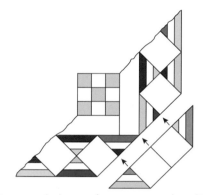

Arrows pointing to where seams need to align

Once these corner pieces are sewn, you can choose how you want to make your quilt square—by adding a piece of your "focus" fabric, by adding a series of strips of color like Carrie did, or by being a little crazy and making your quilt octagonal by leaving the corners off. It's up to you. If you need a reminder of measuring for the corner triangles on a diagonal set quilt, refer to *Quilter's Academy Vol. 2*, Lesson Two (page 23).

We hope you have enjoyed making these first two medallion quilts. Hang in there with us … the fun (and work) is just beginning!

Class 540

The medallion quilts contained in this chapter are not complicated, but will require more time and a more expanded knowledge of many of the basic piecing principles we have covered in the first four volumes of *Quilter's Academy*. These quilts have similar design elements in the quarter-square triangles and Flying Geese, but construction is very different.

We're Going to the Chapel

Quilt top: 98" × 98"

Carrie made this quilt for her and her new husband for their bedroom, and he even helped with the ironing! Carrie has a real love of Log Cabin quilts and has had a stack of coordinating fabric sitting in her sewing area for several years now, waiting for the right quilt to come along. This quilt was inspired by two different quilts Carrie found during one of her long and intensive Internet searches.

One quilt, called *My Story* by Marjorie Jo Mancuso, inspired the star center made from Log Cabin blocks, the three rounds of Log Cabin blocks that are technically the fourth border, and the Flying Geese border.

A website called Amish Country Quilts provided the second image. It too was a Log Cabin with a Flying Geese center, but it had a pieced center that inspired the first through third borders.

Yardage

  1 yard red

  ⅜ yard each of 2 oranges

  ⅝ yard each of 2 yellows

  ½ yard brown

  1 yard each of 5 assorted cream backgrounds

  ½ yard each of 4 assorted greens

  ½ yard each of 4 assorted blues

  1½ yards dark green for plain borders

  3 yards large green floral for outside border

Graph paper plan of quilt

Basics of Design

This quilt is not complicated to construct but is very time consuming due to the large number of Log Cabin blocks that need to be created. This quilt is also square, making it very easy to design and construct, but could easily have been made rectangular with the subtraction of the sixth border on the sides. As it is, it will fit nicely with a 22″ drop on each side of a queen-size mattress and a 24″ drop on the end.

If you are going to make a medallion quilt for a bed, It is good idea to be sure you know the size mattress you will need to be fitting the quilt to and work on designing the center and borders appropriately. In this case the Flying Geese border will just drop off the mattress on the sides and the plain border just toward the center inside the Flying Geese border will be what drops off on the end. The top of the quilt will pull up to the headboard without a pillow tuck so the entire set of border designs of the quilt will be seen at the top of the bed.

Construction

This quilt starts with the construction of 16 little Log Cabin blocks. These blocks have logs that measure ⅝″ finished. Refer back to *Quilter's Academy Vol. 1*, basic Log Cabin block construction (pages 43–46). You will need to cut the strips 1¼″ wide, so that you can trim them down as you go and make your blocks completely accurate in the end.

The only difference between these blocks and the ones covered in *Volume 1* is that they have an uneven number of logs. The dark half has a total of six logs or three per side, while the light half has only four logs, or two per side. There are also two different color variations of these blocks.

Showing the difference between a basic Log Cabin with equal sides and these Log Cabin blocks

Showing the 2 different color variations of the center Log Cabin blocks

The blocks are actually very similar in size and design to the little Log Cabin basket quilt in *Volume 3* (pages 51–53).

Refer to the instructions in either *Volume 1* or *Volume 3* to create the 16 Log Cabin blocks needed. Once you have those done, lay them out in the star pattern shown in the picture, or play around with your design. The 16 Log Cabin blocks can make a number of different designs. The center of your quilt should measure 15½″.

BORDER 1

This is the first of several plain borders that are used to make the following pieced border fit right. This border measures 1″ wide finished and was cut ¼″ wider than the 1½″ cut size to allow for the contraction that is caused by sewing over so many seams in the Log Cabin blocks. Once this border is on, square the corners and trim to size. Your top should now measure 17½″.

BORDER 2

This border is a nod to the look of the second inspiration quilt, even if it doesn't resemble it in overall appearance. This border also is a place where knowing that the fifth border (the 2 rounds of Log Cabin blocks) needed to be a certain size and configuration is helpful. The border had to be adjusted in size to make everything work, so the small colorful spacers were added between the quarter-square triangles to make the border the correct length. Adding another quarter-square triangle would have made the border just a bit too long, and these types of triangles are not ones that look good if they get trimmed off at the end.

The quarter-square triangles are 2½″ finished. Refer to *Quilter's Academy Vol. 3*, Lesson Two (pages 55–57) for how to make these quickly and accurately. The spacers are ¾″ × 2½″ finished measurement, and the half-square triangles in the four corners are also 2½″ square.

Top/Bottom

Sides

Drawings of Border 2

Just as before, you will add the side borders first and then add the top and bottom borders. The addition of this border will make your quilt top measure 22½″.

BORDER 3

This is the second plain border and is the same width as border 1—1″ wide finished.

Attach it the same as you did the other plain border. Square the corners and trim to size, which should be 24½″.

BORDER 4

Here starts the endless sewing of Log Cabin blocks. These blocks are like those in the center—only 4 logs of light color and 6 logs of dark color. There are 2 different color versions of these blocks, just like in the center blocks. These blocks, however, use 1″ finished logs—1⅝″ cut.

Showing the 2 different color variations of the center Log Cabin blocks

You will need a total of 48 blocks, 24 of each of the color variations. Once they are constructed you can lay them out as in the picture of Carrie's quilt. Now your quilt will really start to grow. With these borders added your quilt top should be 48½″ square.

BORDER 5

This is another 1″-wide finished plain border. Because the fabric used for all these borders is a busy paisley print, Carrie cut her strips the width of the fabric (42″) and spliced the strips together to get the length she needed for these borders. The addition of these borders makes the quilt measure 50½″.

BORDER 6

This border is a Log Cabin variation called Courthouse Steps. The Courthouse Steps blocks use a plain border on either side of them as a design element. You will need a total of 32 of these Courthouse Steps blocks. These blocks were created using the same 1″-wide finished measurement, but start with a rectangular center that will measure 1″ × 2″ finished. A square of light is added to each end of this center rectangle.

Beginning of Courthouse Steps block

After the light squares are added and trimmed, you will need to add the longer strips of color again. All of this is done using the same strip-piecing method as for the regular Log Cabin; you are just sewing on two opposite sides of each block rather than in a circle.

Add the next strip to the Courthouse Steps block

Finally, you need to add another short strip of cream to the end of each of these rectangular blocks to complete them. Sew 8 of these rectangular blocks together to create each of the borders.

Adding the final strip to the Courthouse Steps block

To finish this border, 4 cornerstones are needed. Start with a square of one of your lighter colors, then add another square of a darker color. Trim the block and add a second strip of the darker color.

First and second step of cornerstone block

Add a strip of a third color, trim the block, and add a last longer strip of this same color.

Final step of cornerstone block

To finish this border add a second strip of cream to each end of each set of rectangular Courthouse Steps blocks, and add your cornerstones to the end of the top and bottom borders.

Sides

Top/Bottom

Side and top and bottom illustrations of Courthouse Steps border

Once these are attached to the quilt, your top should measure 56½".

BORDER 7

Another plain border is added here, also with a 1"-wide finished measurement. Apply, square your corners, and trim to size. You quilt top should now be 58½".

BORDER 8

This next border is fun to make. If you are using a lot of different fabrics as Carrie did, it is really fun to play with color placement and mixing up the background fabrics. Carrie chose to use the Flying Geese template method covered in *Quilter's Academy Vol. 3*, Lesson Four (pages 71–73). It is fast and easy to create four geese at a time. How you are able to mix up the background color is by using several different squares of background fabric with different-colored squares for the geese and then mixing up the units when you get to Step 3. This will not affect the geese, just the background. You will get two different backgrounds on each goose. If this is too scrappy for you, then just do a large mixture of backgrounds and stay with the instruction for the method. If you find another method for creating Flying Geese more accurate for you, then by all means use that method.

You need a total of 112 – 2" × 4" finished size geese. Carrie chose to put a spacer of one of her main fabrics in the exact middle of each of these borders so that the geese on each side fly into that spot. You can lay your geese out so they circle around the entire quilt, like Harriet has done in *Geese in Flight* (page 72). This is a design element that is entirely up to you.

Diagram of border with spacer

Diagram of border with geese going the same direction

To complete this border there are 4 cornerstones made of 4″ finished half-square triangles, using the same main fabric as the spacer. Add these cornerstones to the top and bottom borders.

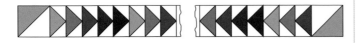

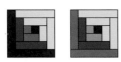

Diagram of border cornerstones added to top and bottom borders

Apply these borders the same as before, side on first, then top and bottom. At this point your quilt top is growing by leaps and bounds and now should measure 66½″ square.

BORDER 9

Here is the last of the interior plain borders. This border is quite a bit wider than the others so that the final Log Cabin border will fit and the blocks will turn the corners correctly. This border measures 3″ finished and was 4″ cut, just to make sure there was a little fudge room once the next border was constructed and measured. Do not pre-trim this border. Leave it as is, until the final pieced border is completed.

BORDER 10

This is the final pieced border. It contains 144 Log Cabin blocks with ¾″ finished strips. These blocks are the same basic construction as the other two sets we have made, but the coloration is a bit different. In these blocks, Carrie wanted to mix up all the colors used in the quilt, but not completely randomly. Look closely at this closeup photo of the drawing she developed as a shorthand way of drafting out the color placement on this final border.

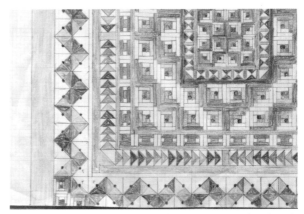

Closeup photo of outer border of *We're Going to the Chapel*

The basic color combinations used are as follows:

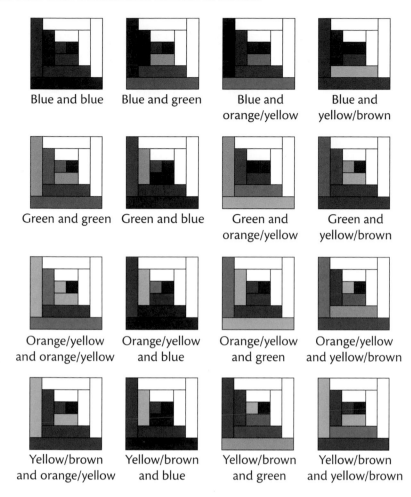

Blue and blue	Blue and green	Blue and orange/yellow	Blue and yellow/brown
Green and green	Green and blue	Green and orange/yellow	Green and yellow/brown
Orange/yellow and orange/yellow	Orange/yellow and blue	Orange/yellow and green	Orange/yellow and yellow/brown
Yellow/brown and orange/yellow	Yellow/brown and blue	Yellow/brown and green	Yellow/brown and yellow/brown

All color combinations

All these color combinations are necessary so that as you are placing the blocks on your design board, at no time will you have the exact same colors next to each other. This process gives this border a sort of sparkle effect, especially where the yellows, oranges, and browns meet.

You can mathematically break down how many of each variation you need like this: 144 ÷ 16 = 9. But if you don't want that many of the yellows, oranges, and browns, make 4 times as many of the blue and green combinations, or 18 each of blue and blue, green and green, blue and green, and green and blue. Then evenly divide the rest. This means you need to make 4 blocks each of the other 12 combinations to make the other 72 blocks. If this seems like too much work, then throw your strips in a paper bag and pull them out as you sew and make them ultra scrappy, similar to what Carrie did with her 1930s baby quilt in *Quilter's Academy Vol. 2*, Lesson Six (page 43).

Once you have all the blocks constructed, sew them into the 2 rows of 16 blocks each for the side borders and 2 rows of 20 blocks each for the top and bottom borders. Attach them to your quilt. Once these borders are added, your quilt should measure 84½″ square.

BORDER 11

The final border on our quilt was the inspiration fabric for the whole thing! This means this border needs to be large enough to really show off! This border was cut 8″ wide and after it was quilted it was trimmed down to 7″ finished.

So there you have it, the largest quilt yet! Certainly the largest quilt Carrie has ever made.

note *Carrie would like to thank Lori Housel for quilting this quilt for her and new husband David. Being still a new quilter, and having never quilted anything this large before, Carrie did not feel confident that she could handle a quilt of this size. Lori is a longarm quilter we have long recommended through our store because of her quality of workmanship, and the fact that she has a Gammill machine with a Statler Stitcher, making it possible for her to completely custom design and quilt to the top maker's desires. That is exactly what she did for Carrie and David. They sat down for about an hour and worked out the quilting designs on each border and for each element of the quilt, so that it would have the look of the quilting Carrie would have done on her own machine. Lori also used Harriet's private-label .004 nylon thread from YLI and Presencia 60/3 on the back. The quilt came back better than Carrie could have imagined, and David and Carrie can't wait to get their bedroom repainted and decorated so this showpiece can have its home on their bed.*

Basic Framed Medallion

Quilt top: 57″ × 57″

A basic medallion with typical components

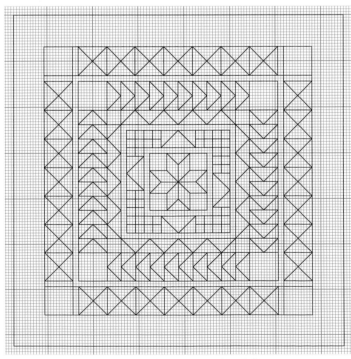

Line drawing of *Basic Framed Medallion*

This quilt was inspired by the framed medallion quilts of the early 1800s. Elements of the quilt include LeMoyne Star, four-patch units, Flying Geese, and quarter-square triangles—all traditional units found in the earliest quilts. All these techniques have been taught in *Quilter's Academy Vol. 1–4*, and we will be referring back to these books for specific instructions for each of the different units in the quilt top. Consider this a warm-up quilt for those coming later in the book.

Yardage

- ½ yard each of 3 different backgrounds
- ⅛ yard dark brown (LeMoyne Star)
- ¼ yard each of 4 different reproduction blues
- ½ yard multicolor floral
- ¼ yard light brown print (triangle border)
- ½ yard brown print for Flying Geese
- ⅛ yard medium/dark brown stripe—first strip border
- ⅛ yard medium/dark brown—second strip border
- ¼ yard dark print—third strip border
- ¼ yard each of 4 different brown prints for quarter-square triangle units
- 1¾ yards stripe for outside border

Basics of Design

To the left is a diagram that breaks the quilt down to the elements in each border. We suggest that you enlarge and photocopy this diagram and color in your fabric selections to give you an idea of how they will play out in each border.

Construction

LEMOYNE STAR BLOCK

LeMoyne Star block

The center of the quilt is a 9″ LeMoyne Star. Any 9″ block can be substituted if you do not care to take the time to construct the star.

For 9″ block, you will need to cut:

❋ 4 – 3⅛″ squares of background

❋ 1 – 5″ square of background, cut into fourths diagonally

❋ 2 – 2⅜″-wide strips, 1 of each fabric, for the star diamonds. Cut 4 – 45° diamonds from each strip, each diamond cut 2⅜″ long.

For complete details of constructing eight-pointed stars, refer to *Quilter's Academy Vol. 4—Senior Year*, Class 440 (pages 52–55). Once the star block is constructed, make sure that it is exactly 9″ point to point both directions, 9½″ square unfinished.

BORDER 1—STRAIGHT STRIP

Now you are ready to add the plain strip that goes between the LeMoyne Star block and the pieced border. This plain border can be cut to accommodate any issues with the size of the LeMoyne Star you may have had. The goal is to have the outside, unfinished measurement of the center be 12½″ square—exactly. The star block and the strip *have* to measure 12½″ unfinished at this point in order for the pieced border to fit correctly. We suggest that you cut the strips wider than you need so that you can trim them to be exactly the needed width.

Cut:

❋ 4 – 2″ × 9½″ strips (or wider and trim) border fabric

❋ 4 – 2″ (or wider and trim) squares for corners

Stitch a strip onto two sides of the LeMoyne Star block. Iron the seam allowance toward the strip. Stitch the squares onto the ends of the remaining strips. Iron the corners toward the strip and attach to the top and bottom

of the star block, butting the corner square seams perfectly. Iron the seams toward the strip.

Center a 12½″ square ruler with the star and align the ruler lines with all the seams to assure that you are square and straight on all four sides. Trim the strips you just added so that the whole unit is exactly 12½″ square.

BORDER 2—FOUR-PATCH AND FLYING GEESE

This is the first pieced border, consisting of 12 four-patch units and 4 – 3″ × 6″ Flying Geese units. The four-patch units are made using 2 fabrics. They are 1½″ finished, cut 2″.

You will need to cut:

❋ 1 – 2″ × 53″ strip of each fabric

Sew the strips together, iron toward the dark, and then cut into 2″ segments. Construct 12 four-patch blocks. Square each block to be exactly 3½″.

You will also need 4 – 3″ × 6″ Flying Geese units. Construct these by any method you prefer. If you need help, we gave four different techniques for making Flying Geese in *Quilter's Academy Vol. 3*, Class 350 (pages 69–75).

Once all the units are made, lay out the pieces around the center unit. The four-patch units are in the corners and the Flying Geese units are in the center. The geese units point outward, forming the appearance of the center's being on point. The four-patch units can mirror one corner to another or all go the same direction. Try both layouts and see which looks best with your fabrics.

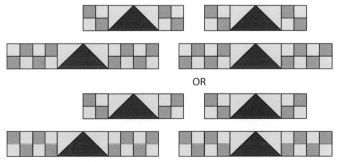

OR

Optional layouts for four-patch units

Once you have made your decision, sew the units together. Starting with the shorter borders, sew a four-patch to each end of the goose units. Iron the four-patch units toward the goose units. Join 2 four-patch units to each other, and repeat to get 4 pairs. Attach one of these units to each end of the goose units.

Add the short pieced borders first, ironing the seam allowance toward the strip. Add the other two sides next, again ironing toward the strip. At this point, the quilt top should be exactly 18½″ square.

BORDER 3—STRAIGHT STRIP

The next border is another plain strip—1″ wide finished. When cutting the strips, add at least ¼″ to the cut measurement to allow for adjusting for the next pieced border.

Cut:

❋ 2 – 1¾″ × 42″ strips

  Subcut into 2 – 19½″-long and 2 – 22″-long border strips.

Stitch the 2 – 19″ strips onto opposite sides of the quilt top. You should have ½″ extending beyond each end. Iron toward the strips and then the square ends. This border should retain the 18½″ measurement in length. Center and pin the remaining two borders into position, again extending the ends ½″. Stitch, iron toward strip, and square ends. You will need to trim the strip to be 1¼″ wide, but first check to see that the center is still square and to size (20½″ raw edge to raw edge). We suggest that you wait to trim until the fourth border is constructed to check for size.

BORDER 4—DOGTOOTH BORDER

Cut:

❋ 8 – 4⅜″ squares background— cut in half diagonally

❋ 10 – 4⅜″ squares medium print— cut in half diagonally

❋ 4 – 3″ squares for corners

tip We can't stress enough how important it is to trim all the corners of the triangles for this border with the Perfect Patchwork Corner Trimmer by Marti Michell. This trimmer allows the points to line up exactly, giving you an accurate seam allowance along the long sides of the border.

Lay out the pieces as in the diagram below. You will need 4 background and 5 medium print triangles in each border. Sew the triangles into pairs, and then join them all together. Iron the seams very carefully, as you are dealing with a lot of bias along the edges. It is helpful to iron the seams so that the seam intersections show as much as possible to help you hit the points when attaching the border.

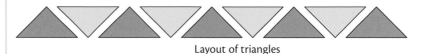

Layout of triangles

The triangles at the ends of each border will be cut off once the border is ironed and measured. Each strip must measure 21½″ at this point.

Cutting ends

Pin and sew two of these units to the sides of the quilt center, background fabric edge to the quilt top (see illustration below). Iron the seam allowance toward the plain strip.

Border placement

Attach the corner squares onto the ends of the remaining two borders. Iron the seam toward the square. Pin and sew these borders to the quilt center, matching the seam intersections. Iron the seam allowance toward the plain strip.

Check the quilt for being square again. At this point, the quilt top should be 25½" square. If it is smaller than that, an optional strip border can be added here to bring the top up to size for the Flying Geese border. We suggest that you not do anything about this until the Flying Geese border is constructed, as the actual measurements may vary from the mathematically correct ones.

BORDER 5— FLYING GEESE

This border is made with 40 – 2½" × 5" (finished) Flying Geese units, 10 on each side of the quilt. Use any method you prefer for making the Flying Geese. We prefer to work with Harriet's Flying Geese Templates because of the extreme accuracy as taught in *Quilter's Academy Vol. 3*, Class 350, Lesson Four (pages 71–73).

If you choose this method, you will need to cut:

❋ 10 – 8" squares light background fabric

❋ 10 – 6½" squares goose fabric

Once the Flying Geese are constructed, join 10 in a row for each border. The length of these borders should fit the sides of your quilt top. If they are too long, the extra strip we discussed above can be added to increase the size of the quilt top in order to accommodate the borders.

Attach two borders on opposite sides of the quilt top, being careful not to cut off any points. Check that the geese arc flying in opposite directions. Carefully iron seams toward the fourth border. Add the corner squares to the 2 remaining geese borders and attach to the remaining sides of the quilt top. Iron carefully.

BORDER 6— STRAIGHT STRIP

This border is another plain strip, 1" wide finished. Repeating the process we did for the third border, cut the strips wider than needed, measure to length through the center of the quilt top, and cut to length plus 1". Center, pin, and let ½" extend beyond the edge of the quilt top on each end. Stitch, being careful not to cut off any geese points. Iron toward strip and then add the remaining two sides.

BORDER 7— QUARTER-SQUARE TRIANGLES

The final pieced border is made of quarter-square triangles. Instructions for making these can be found in *Quilter's Academy Vol. 3*, Class 340, Lesson Two (pages 55 and 56).

These units need to be 5" finished, 5½" cut.

You will need to cut:

❋ 14 – 6½" squares background fabric

❋ 14 – 6½" squares various darker prints

Be sure that when you square the blocks the seams are exactly in the corners. Marsha McCloskey's Precision Trimmer 6 is our favorite ruler for trimming to exact sizes.

Lay out the blocks in the desired color arrangement. You will be stitching 7 blocks together per side.

Color arrangement for quarter-square blocks

You will find that this border is not long enough to fit the edges of the quilt top at this point. When drafting this quilt design, we found that if the blocks were large enough to fit the given length of the quilt top, the blocks were too big and bulky—out of proportion to the rest of the top. The way around this is to add a spacer to the ends of the borders to gain the needed extra length.

Cut:

❋ 8 – 1½" × 5½" strips of the background fabric used in the quarter-square triangle blocks

Attach a strip to each end of the border strips. This measurement can be adjusted to fit your actual measurements once the plain strip is trimmed. Iron the seam allowance toward the spacer.

Sew the borders onto the quilt top.

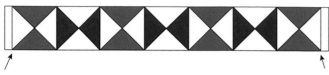

Attaching spacers to the ends of borders

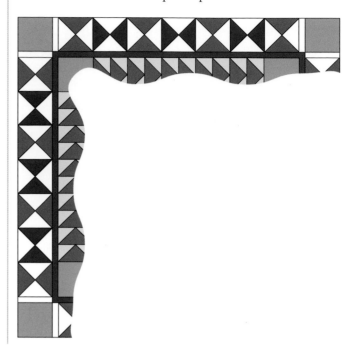

Cut:

❊ 4 – 5½″ squares for corner squares. Attach them to the ends of 2 of the borders.

Before adding these borders, trim the plain Border 6 to 1¼″. The length of the quarter-square blocks and the spacers should equal the length of the quilt top once this is trimmed. Adjust the trimming amount to make these two measurements match if necessary.

BORDER 8— FINAL BORDER

The final border can be any width you think looks good on your top. This can change considerably with the color, busyness, and pattern of the fabric you have selected. Audition the fabric at different widths and go with what you think looks best. We always suggest that the final border be cut a couple of inches wider than needed to aid in the quilting process. The excess is trimmed away once the quilting is finished.

The quilting on this quilt is quite heavy and very true to how the original medallion quilts were quilted. Here is a line drawing illustration of how Harriet quilted this quilt top.

Typical quilting ideas for a framed medallion

Basic Frame
Medallion Variations

Harriet's version of this quilt
using the same fabric collection as Carrie

Carrie's version of this quilt
using the same fabric collection as Harriet

While team teaching this quilt at a retreat, we were seeing some of the tops telling the student to stop. No matter what we tried, the quilt seemed to be finished, even though there were borders left to add. That sent us to wanting to play with the idea of using the same fabrics in different ways and experience how the tops would progress. Carrie's stopped much sooner than Harriet's did. The center of Carrie's quilt reads very light compared with Harriet's. Once the Flying Geese were added to Carrie's center, the addition of anything else seemed to overpower it. The Flying Geese in Harriet's quilt are lighter than the brown in the center, so it remained balanced and able to handle more borders. Perhaps if we had had more fabrics to work with, Carrie's quilt could have continued; but with a limited palette, this is where the quilt said to stop.

Carrie also wanted to make this quilt in the same color palette as the original but with modern prints. Notice how the quilt changes. This version is still an elegant quilt, but a long way from the basic medallion where we started. The possibilities are endless.

Carrie's modern fabric version of the original quilt

Class 550

We are continuing with quilts that take more time and are a bit more complicated than those before this chapter. *Fancy Tail Feathers* was completely inspired by the beautiful fabric. Instead of a panel, the center was cut from yardage. Cutting an elongated center as well as taking off the corners presented some new challenges in the construction. *Peppermint Delight* takes us back to *Volumes 2* and *3,* where we introduced you to Internal Frames. This classy Christmas quilt is made totally from blocks, but because of the magic of Internal Frames, the quilt takes on the appearance of a medallion.

This quilt was inspired by the peacock fabric Carrie fussy cut for the center.

This is the type of fabric we were talking about in Class 520 (page 22) when discussing different types of fabrics that could be used as centers of medallions—something with a very large motif that can be fussy cut.

Fancy Tail Feathers

Quilt top size: 70″ × 80″

Basics of Design

When Carrie saw this fabric, the only idea she had was that she wanted to create a different-shaped center and a checkerboard of four-patches somewhere in the design. The colors and the rest of the design evolved. The colors came from a search of our store's fabric selection, trying to find colors that matched or blended with those of the peacock print. This led into the shades and hues of creams, browns, grays, and blacks that are present in the quilt. These neutral colors when laid out as a collection don't seem to have much to do with each other, but when cut up in little pieces in a quilt, and this quilt in particular, they work very well together. This is something that Mary Mashuta used to call *pushed neutrals*, a concept of taking a few basic neutral colors and working in many of the hues and tones of those neutrals to create a very warm and balanced palette for your quilt.

The other half of the inspiration was the coordinating border print. The yardage had two different stripes across the width. Both were used—one around the center medallion and the second (the flowers) as the outer border. The quilt needed to be able to work in both size and appearance so that these preprinted borders would fit in with the overall quilt design. The last element of inspiration was an obscure picture in one of Harriet's quilt books of a four-patch on-point border. It is found in the fifth border. All these elements were combined in an organic idea that eventually created this quilt.

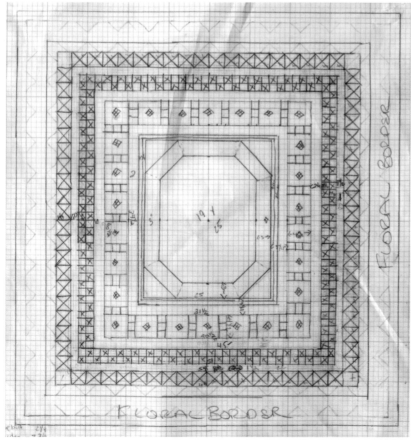

Line drawing of *Fancy Tail Feathers*

Yardage

1 yard at least for center panel; Be sure there is enough fabric on each side as well as above and below the motif you are wanting to use to accommodate the size you are needing to cut. Take a tape measure to the quilt shop when purchasing your fabric if necessary.

5 fat quarters in varying hues and shades of at least 4 different colors; In Carrie's case there were 5 grays, 5 blacks, 5 browns, 5 tans, and 5 creams.

For the fabrics that will be the solid borders you will need:

⅛ yard for border 2

¼ yard for border 3

⅔ yard for borders 4 and 10

½ yard for border 6

½ yard for border 8

¼ yard each of 2 other colors for border 10

1⅛ yards of cream used in border 5

2¼ yards or more, depending on size, of border stripe; You need the length of the quilt plus two times the width of the border so you will have enough fabric to create the miter at each corner.

Construction

As mentioned before, Carrie didn't want the center of this quilt to be square or rectangular as in the rest of the quilts covered in this book. So, the decision was made to make this an elongated octagon. This is done by first deciding on a size that fits the motif you are cutting out. For this quilt the rectangle was originally cut 19½″ × 25½″.

Fold he rectangle in half in both directions and iron to mark the centerline both horizontally and vertically. To create the octagon shape, measure from the center on the top and bottom, over 5″ in each direction and make a mark in each of these two locations, both on the top and bottom of your center.

From the center point on the sides, measure up and down 8″ and make a mark in each direction. With these marks being made, line up your long ruler with the 45° line along an edge and make your cut. Repeat this for each of the four corners. The top and bottom from point to point should measure 10″, the side should measure 16″, and the diagonal cuts should measure 7″.

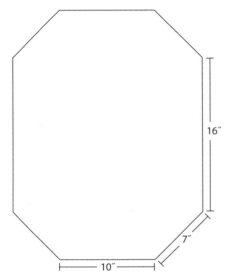

Diagram of octagon showing measurements

BORDER 1

One of the preprinted border stripes was added to the octagon shape for the border. This stripe measured 3″ wide finished. Find a centering line of your chosen border stripe and line up the 1¾″ line of your ruler with that centering line. This allows for the finished width of the stripe plus seam allowance. Cut along the side of the border stripe and

then turn the fabric around and cut the other side. From these long border strips (they are the length of your cut yardage, in this case 2⅛ yards), you will need to cut the segments for the eight sides of your octagon.

To figure the length of these segments, you need the length of the edge of the octagon plus the diagonal measurement of the width of the stripe, in this case 3″ × 1.414 = 4¼″, plus about 1″ extra for safety. The diagonal measurement of the stripe is needed because you are going to be sewing each stripe down across the diagonal length of the stripe below it.

In this case you need:

❀ 4 segments 7″ + 4.25″ + 1″ = 12¼″ each, or a total of 49″ of stripe

❀ 2 segments 10″ + 4.25″ + 1″ = 15¼″ each, or a total of 30½″ of stripe

❀ 2 segments 16″ + 4.25″ + 1″ = 21¼″ each, or a total of 42½″ of stripe

This makes a total of 122″ needed, or 3⅜ yards, or 2 border stripes the length of your yardage.

To create the spinning effect of this innermost border, start with the top of your octagon, pin one of the 15¼″ segments to the octagon, overlapping one end of the strip past where you start sewing by about ¾″. Stop sewing about 2″ from the next corner of the octagon—mark this point with a pin if necessary.

Next, align one of the 12¼″ strip segments along the diagonally cut side of the octagon, again overlapping the end a little before you start sewing. Sew 2″ from the next corner.

There are two ways to proceed. You can keep progressing in this fashion, sewing the border strip segments to your octagon, and then go back and trim and complete the seams. Or you can stop here, iron the strip you just added, lay a ruler down parallel with first seam you sewed, trim off any excess fabric, and then go back to your sewing machine and complete this seam, then iron. If you choose to add a strip at a time, you will always add a strip to one side of your octagon, stop 2″ from the corner, then iron and trim the strip you sewed just previous, and complete the seam. This is very much like the technique we did in

Quilter's Academy Vol. 4, Lesson One (page 92) for making blocks with partial seams.

Adding first strip to octagon center

Trimming and completing the seam after second strip is added to octagon center

Trimming and completing the seam after third strip is added to octagon center

Once you have made it all the way around the octagon you will need to add the corner triangles to the diagonal sides of the octagon to make it rectangular again. You can determine the size triangle you need by laying a square ruler down with the 45° line on the diagonal side of your octagon and adjusting it to measure the square corner. Take the measurement you get (Carrie got 6½″), add

1½″, cut 2 squares that size, and then cut those in half diagonally. Add these triangles to your corners, and square your whole center up with a large square ruler.

BORDERS 2, 3, AND 4
All three of these borders are plain fabric borders.

❋ Border 2 measures ½″ wide finished and is cream.

❋ Border 3 measures ¾″ and is tan.

❋ Border 4 measures 2″ finished and is black.

When all these borders are added, squared, and trimmed, your quilt center should measure 32″ × 38″. The last of these borders is wider than the other two and would be a place to adjust width if necessary, so you may not want to trim Border 4 until you have Border 5 made.

BORDER 5
This is a fun border that adds a bit of sparkle to a quilt with its floating little four-patches.

You will need to make 26 – 1¼″ finished four-patches. These little four-patches are then surrounded in Courthouse Steps, Log Cabin fashion, with strips of cream background fabric cut 1⅜″ wide. You will add short strips to the two opposite sides of the four-patches, iron, and then add two longer strips to the remaining two sides. Iron and measure from these seams, trimming down to 1″ wide. To complete this part of these blocks you will need 7 – 1⅜″ strips of your background fabric.

You may want to refer to *Quilter's Academy Vol. 3*, Lesson Three (page 38) for making a square-in-a-square block. These blocks need to end up finishing 4½″ square, or 5″ cut. Carrie chose to make her triangles large and trim away the excess to ensure accuracy with her finished blocks. She cut 6 – 4½″ strips of background and subcut those into 52 – 4½″ squares, which were then cut in half diagonally.

When all four triangles are added and ironed around the four-patch blocks, trim them to size. Refer to the following photo for a guide on how to align your ruler to do this quickly and accurately.

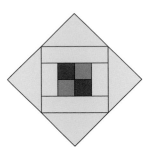

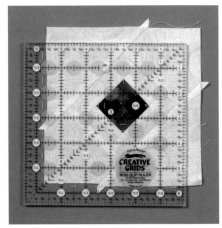

Trimming blocks to size

The second part of this border is separator strips. These are made up of 3 – 1½" (finished size) squares. You need a total of 26 of these strips.

To prepare this border to add to the quilt, alternate the separator strips and blocks. For the side borders you need 7 strips and 6 blocks. For the top and bottom borders you need 6 strips and 7 blocks.

Sides

Top & Bottom

Side, top, and bottom border configurations

BORDER 6

This is another plain fabric border from a different black than was used in Border 4. This border again equalizes the size of the quilt in preparation of the next border. The top and bottom borders finish at 2⅛", were cut 3" wide, and trimmed to a width of 2⅜". The side borders finish at 1⅛", were cut 2¾", and trimmed to 1⅜" once Border 7 was made and measured.

BORDER 7

This border is composed of 2½" finished scrappy quarter-square triangles. The quilt now measures 43" × 50½". Border 6 was used to make the quilt measurement a "happy" measurement for this quarter-square triangle border. For the sides, you will need 20 quarter-square blocks; for the top and bottom borders, you will need 19 quarter-square triangle blocks each. Use your favorite method for creating the 78 quarter-square triangle blocks you need for this border. For a refresher, refer back to *Quilter's Academy Vol. 3*, Lesson Two (page 55).

BORDER 8

This is another plain fabric border from the same black used in Border 4. This border is another "equalizing border," again with different widths for the sides as for the top and bottom so that the next border will fit properly. The side borders finish at 1½" and cut at 2"; the top and bottom borders finish at 2" and cut at 2½".

BORDER 9

This is a very scrappy checkerboard border made up of bunches of four-patches. You will need a total of 78 four-patches that measure 3" square when finished. Of these, 20 will be attached to each side and 19 will also be attached to your top and bottom border.

BORDER 10

The quilt now measures 57½" × 66½". This next to last border is a narrow plain fabric border of black that finishes at ½" wide.

BORDER 11

To create this border you will need to tear off four border stripes the longest length of your quilt plus two times the width of the border stripe. In this case, the quilt now measures 59" × 67", and the border stripe is 6" wide. To find the length needed, use the equation 67" + (2 × 6") = 79". The extra length is to ensure you have enough fabric to miter the corners. Follow the instructions in *Quilter's Academy Vol. 1*, Lesson Four (page 98) for attaching and mitering this border. You've made it to the outer edge!

This quilt has a very contemporary and classy feel. It could just as easily be a sports theme or use a children's panel, a wildlife picture, or any other theme that would look stunning on your wall!

Peppermint Delight

Quilt top: 78″ × 78″

This quilt is a little different than all the other quilts covered in this book. It's not that it isn't a medallion, but the borders are created by a series of pieced blocks, not strips of fabric or blocks sewn as a strip. We talked about incorporated borders in both *Volumes 2* and *3*, and in this quilt we are using them as the sole design element in creating the medallion-looking borders. If you are rusty on making a diagonal-set quilt, be sure to have your copy of *Quilter's Academy Vol. 2* nearby.

Yardage:

3¾ yards cream background*

1 yard red

1 yard green

2 yards focus fabric for outer border

One or more fabrics can be used for each of the three main colors to add interest and depth to each of the incorporated borders.

Construction

This quilt starts with a single 9″ block in its center. We used the Yankee Puzzle block as the center, but you could pick any of the blocks pictured in *Quilter's Academy Vol. 3*, Lesson Seven (page 18) or any other block, just so long as it has a pinwheel effect.

You will also want to refer to *Volume 3* and pick your favorite method for creating the 16 half-square triangles you need to make from the cream and red fabrics.

Lay them out according to your chosen block layout or like the illustration below for Yankee Puzzle.

Yankee Puzzle

BORDER 1

This border is made from four corner incorporated-border blocks.

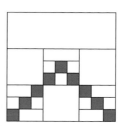

Border 1, corner incorporated-border block

This block has four basic elements: a long plain strip of the cream fabric, two plain squares of the cream fabric, and two different pieced nine-patch variation blocks made with the cream and green fabrics.

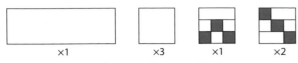

Four elements of Border 1 blocks

If you need help figuring out how to piece these nine-patch blocks, refer back to Harriet's *Double Nine-Patch Chain* quilt. Instructions for making the nine-patch blocks you need are illustrated in *Volume 1*, Class 160 (page 78).

You will need a total of:

❋ 4 – 3½″ × 9½″ rectangles of cream

❋ 12 – 3½″ squares of cream

❋ 4 – 1½″ × 3½″ rectangles of cream

❋ At least 6″ of a strip set of 1½″ cut strips of green, cream, and green

❋ At least 18″ of a strip set of 1½″ cut strips of cream, green, and cream

❋ At least 24″ of a strip set of a 2½″ strip of cream and a 1½″ strip of green

Once you have these four blocks assembled, lay them out with your center square. Don't worry about sewing all the squares together; we will do that at the very end.

BORDER 2

The second border of this quilt is really what gave the quilt its name. There are 4 corner blocks and 4 side blocks.

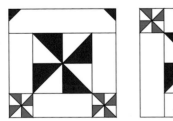

Corner and side blocks for Border 2

To create the corner blocks, you will need:

❋ 4 – 2½″ × 9½″ rectangles of cream

❋ 12 – 2½″ × 5½″ rectangles of cream

❋ 16 – 2½″ finished size red and cream half-square triangles, made using your favorite method

❋ 32 – 1″ finished size green and cream half-square triangles, use your favorite method again

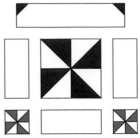

Corner block elements ready to be attached to each other

For the side blocks, you will need:

❋ 2 – 2″ squares cut in half diagonally. These are for the red tips that intersect the next border. (If you need a refresher on making Snowball-type blocks, refer to *Volume 3*, Lesson Four, page 39, for how to do this.)

❋ 8 – 2½″ × 7½″ rectangles of cream

❋ 8 – 2½″ × 5½″ rectangles of cream

❋ 16 – 2½″ finished size, red and cream half-square triangles, made using your favorite method

❋ 32 – 1″ finished size green and cream half-square triangles, using your favorite method

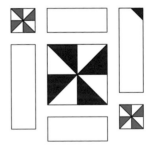

Side block elements ready to be attached to each other

Once these blocks are completed, you can position them on your design wall and get ready for the next border.

BORDER 3

This cute little border has many little snowball tips to add to squares and rectangles. As we add borders, we are adding blocks. There are still 4 corners, but now there are 8 side blocks.

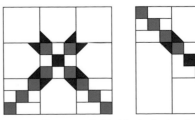

Corner and side blocks for border 3

To create the corner blocks, you will need:

❋ 24 – 3½" squares of cream;
Of these, 8 will be plain; on the other 16 you will add triangle corners to 2 adjacent corners.

❋ 16 – 2" squares of red, cut in half diagonally for snowball corners

❋ At least 12" of a strip set of 1½" cut strips of green, cream, and green

❋ At least 6" of a strip set of 1½" cut strips of cream, red, and cream

❋ At least 24" of a strip set of a 2½" cut strip of cream and a 1½" cut strip of green

❋ At least 12" of a strip set of 1½" cut strips of cream, green, and cream

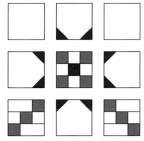

Corner block elements ready to be attached to each other

For the side blocks, you will need:

❋ 16 – 3½" × 6½" rectangles of cream;
Each will need a red triangle on one corner. *Pay close attention to the layout of which corner gets that red tip.*

❋ 16 – 3½" squares of cream;
Each will need a red triangle on one corner.

❋ 16 – 2" squares of red, cut in half diagonally for snowball corners

❋ At least 12" of a strip set of 1½" cut strips of green, cream, and green

❋ At least 6" of a strip set of 1½" cut strips of cream, red, and cream

❋ At least 24" of a strip set of a 2½" strip of cream and a 1½" strip of green

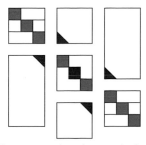

Side block elements ready to be attached to each other

One more round of blocks completed. Just two more to go!

BORDER 4

This is a "plain" border. It is made up of just square blocks, some of which will have small red triangles in one corner in order to complete the last border's design. This is a place where you can show off some quilting or appliqué if you choose.

For this border you will need a total of 16 – 9½" squares. Of these squares, 12, those on the sides, will each get a single red triangle on one corner. You will need to cut 6 – 2" squares of red, cut them in half diagonally, and attach them to one corner.

Side blocks with red triangle attached

When you lay these blocks out, the red tip goes toward the last border you constructed, and the completely plain blocks are placed in each of the 4 corners. Refer to the graph paper drawing of this quilt below to see the block orientation to help you lay out these and the remaining blocks on your design wall.

Drawing of *Peppermint Delight*

BORDER 5

This is a classy border you can add to just about any diagonally set quilt, and despite the color change, it is a relatively easy border to create, especially after making all the tiny pinwheels and nine-patches for the other borders!

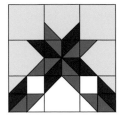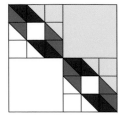

Corner and side blocks for Border 5

Start again with the corner blocks. There are fewer of them, but they are a little more complicated to piece so get them out of the way first.

To create corner blocks, you will need a total of:

❊ 20 – 3½″ squares of background fabric;
Of these, 8 will be plain and 12 will receive a red triangle on one corner and a green triangle on the adjacent corner. *Again, pay close attention to the color placement of these.* You will want the colors to align properly when you make the center of these corner blocks.

❊ 4 – 3½″ squares of cream;
Each will have the same colored triangles, in the same orientation as the squares of background fabric.

❊ 8 – 2½″ squares of green cut in half diagonally;
This yields enough triangles for both the background and cream squares.

❊ 8 – 2½″ squares of red cut in half diagonally;
This yields enough triangles for both the background and cream squares.

❊ 24 – 1½″ finished half-square triangles red and green

❊ 4 – 1½″ finished half-square triangles red and cream

❊ 4 – 1½″ finished half-square triangles green and cream

❊ 4 – 1½″ finished half-square triangles red and background fabric

❊ 4 – 1½″ finished half-square triangles green and background fabric

Once all your different elements are made, refer to the following illustration for placement and sewing.

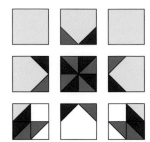

Corner block elements ready to be attached to each other

The side blocks for this border are much easier to construct than the corner blocks.

For side blocks, you will need a total of:

❊ 16 – 5″ squares of background

❊ 16 – 5″ squares of cream

❊ 64 – 1½″ finished half-square triangles red and green

❊ 32 – 1½″ finished half-square triangles red and cream

❊ 32 – 1½″ finished half-square triangles green and cream

❊ 32 – 1½″ finished half-square triangles red and background fabric

❊ 32 – 1½″ finished half-square triangles green and background fabric

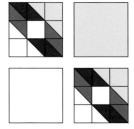

Side block elements ready to be attached to each other

That's its for blocks! Once you have these laid out around the outside of all your other blocks, you are ready to cut your side-setting and corner triangles from your background fabric. The yardage for this quilt was figured on cutting 5 – 14½″ squares and then cutting those in half twice diagonally. The corner squares were cut from 2 – 11″ squares, cut in half once diagonally. We hope you have enjoyed this foray into making an unconventional medallion quilt.

Class 560

The quilts in this chapter are here to put not only your design skills to work, but also your piecing skills. While on a whole they are not overly complicated in their piecework, each of these quilts, during construction, must be handled carefully. You will be working with large amounts of bias, which can at times be your friend, but at other times can work against you if not handled well. This was the challenge, especially with *A Sunny Day in the Park*. Carrie quickly found that this was a quilt that she could not hang on the design wall for extended periods of time because it would stretch and behave very badly when it came time to add a border. A lot of starch, and the extra patience of Harriet, was needed to make this quilt turn out the way it did. Harriet and Carrie encountered similar issues with the *Colorado Memories* quilt with the outer pieced border. All these types of problems can be solved, with patience, perseverance, and lots of starch! These are the types of problems that, once encountered and handled, give you a sense of empowerment as a quilter. You will feel that you can tackle just about anything. And if worse comes to worst and something just won't lie completely flat even though it measures right, many times those issues can be camouflaged with quilting.

A Sunny Day in the Park

Quilt top: 86″ × 98″

The moral of the story? Don't let these quilts intimidate you—they aren't that hard. Just be patient with them and with yourself, and if you get frustrated, walk away for a while. Remember you are working on a masterpiece here, not just a quilt for a college dorm room.

This is another quilt that Carrie designed for her bedroom … but it was in process long before she met David. The Lone Star in the middle of Carrie's quilt was a block made when taking Harriet's *Art of Classic Quiltmaking* series of classes at the store, when that book, not the *Quilter's Academy* series, was the standard beginning quilt textbook at Harriet's shop. Carrie had also collected all the fabrics at that time and just held onto them and the block, waiting for the right quilt design. So here it is!

Yardage:

7 assorted fat quarters for Lone Star block

¾ yard each of 5 or more assorted blues

¾ yard each of 5 or more assorted greens

2½ yards light yellow print

1 yard green paisley

1 yard bright yellow tonal

¼ yard light blue floral

2 yards white print

1 yard bright blue for borders

3¼ yards blue butterfly print for outer border

Construction

This quilt, as mentioned before, started with the construction of the center Lone Star block. This block measures 24″ finished. At this point and with a block and quilt like this, it is absolutely necessary that you make sure all of your corners are 100% square and straight. The methods used to put this quilt together will cause any squareness issues to multiply as you get further out from the center.

BORDER 1

The first border is a plain fabric border sewn around the center block to really accentuate the block and make it the star of the show. This is a border that you cannot trim down until the entire middle of your quilt is constructed. This will come in handy if you find that the block units that surround the center are a little larger or smaller than planned. Carrie's borders were cut 2″ and trimmed down so they finished at 1″. Be sure to work with your own measurement for this border.

BORDER 2

For the sake of ease, Border 2 is the large green triangle. The edges of half-square triangles make the on-point center into a rectangular quilt. You need 40 – 2″ finished half-square triangles for this border as well as 4 – 2½″ cut size squares of green for cornerstones.

Also cut 8 triangles of yellow that are a little oversized. Start with 3¼″ squares and cut them in half diagonally. Construct the strips of half-square triangles as shown:

×4   ×4

Half-square triangle strips

Once you have the strips of half-square triangles constructed, add one of the single yellow triangles to the blue triangle at the end of each strip. Refer to the following illustration for orientation of these triangles if necessary. Measuring the shorter of the two sets of strips, cut 2 – 11″ squares of the green. Cut them in half diagonally. Sew the short sets of triangle strips onto a short side of each of the green triangles, and then add the other long sets of triangle strips as shown.

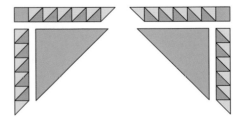

Right and left large triangles with triangle strips being added

Once the triangle strips are added, you can trim the entire unit to be a 14⅞″ triangle.

BORDER 3

This border is composed of 3-piece triangle pinwheel blocks. Construction of these blocks is covered in detail in *Quilter's Academy Vol. 3*, Lesson Three, Method Two (pages 57–61). The blocks measure 6½″ when finished, making each 3-piece triangle unit measure 3¾″ cut size. You need 18 blocks, 9 with blue pinwheels and 9 with green pinwheels.

While it appears that this is a border, it is actually constructed in large triangular units that attach to the center square.

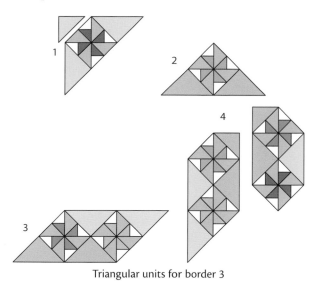

Triangular units for border 3

To make these units, you need to first get the side-setting and corner triangles cut and attached. You need 10 blue side-setting triangles and 4 corner triangles. You also need 18 yellow side-setting triangles and 4 corner triangles.

Attach these to the pinwheel blocks as shown in the following illustrations:

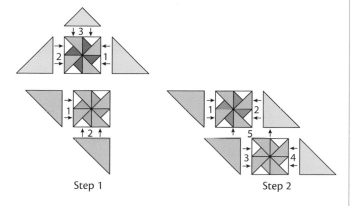

Step 1   Step 2

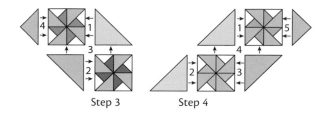

Step 3   Step 4

Adding corner and side-setting triangles
to blocks, creating units

Once you have these four basic units made, attach them to the large green triangle unit. This is a bit like putting a puzzle back together.

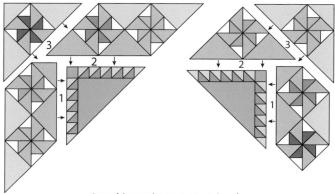

Attaching units to green triangle

Once you have the units attached to the green triangle you can attach the triangles to the center square.

Attaching triangle units to center square

Finally, add the last of the units to the corners of your quilt top. At this point, if all has gone well your quilt top should measure 46½″ × 55¾″.

BORDER 4

Here is another plain fabric border for you to manipulate the size of, if needed. This border will finish at 1½". Again, cut it wider than 2" to be able to trim to adjust if necessary.

BORDER 5

The next-to-last pieced border is made of four-patch blocks set on point. The chain is created by choosing the greens and blues randomly and making it very scrappy. The four-patches are 4" cut, 3½" finished, with a diagonal measurement of 5" when finished. Follow the instructions in Class 590 (page 115) for how to easily attach the side-setting triangles by using rectangles. This makes for a bias edge on this border. If handled carefully it shouldn't cause you any problems. Be careful with aggressive ironing and pulling.

BORDER 6

We are back to another narrow plain fabric border. The top and bottom border is wider than the sides to make the following border fit properly. The side borders finish at 1" and the top and bottom borders finish at 1½". This border needs to be cut to size so that the next border, one of alternating triangles, can be accurately fitted to the quilt. With this addition and the squaring and trimming of this border, your quilt top should measure 62" × 73⅝".

BORDER 7

While this looks like three separate borders, it is actually part of a single design. The triangles for each of the alternating triangle borders need to be 2" wide when measured diagonally, and 3⅞" on the long part of the triangle.

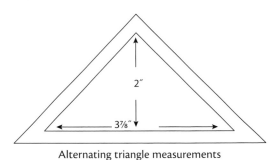

Alternating triangle measurements

For the side borders you need 17 full green triangles and 2 half green triangles, one at each end* of the border row, and 18 full yellow triangles.

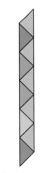

End each triangle border row with full triangle

For the top and bottom borders you will need 15 full green triangles and 2 half green triangles, one at each end* of the border row, and 16 full yellow triangles.

When you construct these borders, sew on an entire triangle and trim it in half later, because with seam allowance it ends up being a little more than half a triangle.

You will also need to construct 4 half-square triangle units that are 2" finished, from your yellow and green fabrics.

Work on a large flat surface, preferably your ironing board if you have a Big Board. Find the center and end points of your border. Pin in place. Measure and mark your ¼" seam allowance on both the end of the triangle border and the plain fabric border, and draw lines indicating the seamline and the cutting line on the end triangles.

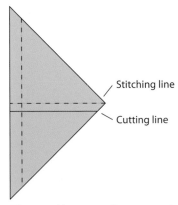

Lines marking seam allowance and cutting lines of end triangle

If the border is a little large, spray with starch and delicately shrink up the fullness in the triangles. This is the beauty of bias: it will work with you and the starch to fit. Once your border is pinned securely in place, sew it on and repeat for the other side.

For the top and bottom borders, you will need to add the half-square triangle units at the ends of each. You will again want to measure the seam and cutting lines and be sure everything is in alignment before you cut off the end triangle. Once these units are added, carry through with the same process you did with the side borders if necessary. Iron the seam allowance gently toward the plain fabric border.

Add the plain fabric border that is in the middle of this border set. This strip needs to measure 2″ finished. These borders need to be cut to length, with ½″ added at each end to ensure you are controlling the bias edges of the triangles. Measure through the center of your quilt carefully and then add the ½″ for each end. Find the center of this border and pin it in place, then pin the ends securely as well. You will again need to repeat the process you just did with the pinning and starching, if necessary. Same procedure as before, sides first, then top and bottom.

Finally, you can construct the outer part of this dogtooth border. Your quilt should now measure 70½″ × 81⅝″. You will need 20 full yellow triangles, 19 full blue triangles, and 2 half blue triangles for each of the side borders, and 18 full yellow triangles, 17 full blue triangles, and 2 half-triangles for the top and bottom borders. You also need 4 more half-square triangles made from yellow and blue that measure 2″ finished. Same game as the other set of these borders: carefully position, pin (shrink if necessary), and sew these borders onto your quilt.

BORDER 8

You've reached the outer border! You will have to do the same manipulation with the triangles you have done twice before, but this is the last time. This border also needs to be cut to the exact width and length of your quilt so that the bias edge of the triangle borders can be controlled. Measure carefully and cut your sides first, sew them on, then measure again from side to side for the size of the top and bottom borders.

Carrie's borders on this quilt were cut 7½″, trimmed down to 6½″ when finished.

Congratulations on completing a quilt that is really easier to construct than it looks!

Colorado Memories

Quilt top: 63″ × 80″

Harriet and Carrie created this quilt for the Denver metro area's 2010 Shop Hop. The block patterns in the outer border were selected individually by the seven participating shops and were made by each shop in two different colorways. The challenge in Carrie's mind was to somehow design a quilt that was not your run-of-the-mill blocks and sashing and would truly showcase the fourteen blocks. This quilt is the end result. It had to be designed from the outside in, making it a different challenge than most quilters encounter, but is something that fits the idea of a medallion perfectly. When you have a set amount of space, how do you fill it? This is a fun quilt to make, please enjoy!

Yardage

- 14 – 9″ finished pieced blocks with designs and colors of your choosing

- 14 or more assorted fat eighths or fat quarters in a variety of colors and patterns

- 2 yards of cream solid for background of blocks

- 1½ yards of dark Colorado toile

- 2¼ yards of light Colorado toile

- 4¼ yards brown for sashings and borders

Construction

Even though this quilt was designed from the outside in, it still has to be constructed from the center out. For our quilt we used a specially printed toile that was available in 2010 for the Denver metro area Shop Hop. Several scenes that depicted iconic scenery in Colorado were printed on the fabric, so the center square of this quilt is fussy cut with the Colorado State Capitol Building centered in the 9″ square. You will want to use an equally iconic or interesting fabric for this quilt.

BORDER 1

The first border is a dogtooth border. You will need to cut 4 – 2″ squares of four different colors, as well as 6 – 2½″ squares of different colors. Cut the 2½″ squares in half diagonally to make 12 half-square triangles. Also, cut 8 – 2½″ squares of the cream solid and cut them in half diagonally to create 16 half-square triangles.

Refer to Class 590 (page 115) for the construction process.

Construct two of each of the alternating triangle borders as shown in the following illustration.

Side and top and bottom diagram of border 1

Sew the two short borders to two opposite sides of the center square and then add the other two borders to the remaining sides. The center of your quilt should now measure 12″.

BORDER 2

This is a plain border but uses one of the toile fabrics. It could be cut from any fabric that is complementary to your center square. Cut 2 strips of the light toile 3″ wide and use these strips to create the plain border around the center medallion. Your center should now measure 17″.

BORDER 3

This isn't a border per se, but it does serve to create a square frame around your on-point center square. Construct 8 of the multi-triangle units that surround the center medallion.

Diagram of the multipoint triangle units

Each of these units is made from 6 scrappy half-square triangles and 4 single triangles. The half-square triangles finish to be 1½″. Cut 24 – 3″ squares of both the cream solid and assorted-color prints. Use your favorite method for making multiple triangles from *Quilter's Academy Vol. 3*, Class 310 (page 5) and Class 320 (page 19).

Construct 8 units to look like those shown in the previous illustration.

The second element of this "border" is the 4 Puss-in-the-Corner blocks.

For these you will need:

- ❋ 16 – 2″ colored squares
- ❋ 16 – 2″ × 3½″ rectangles of light toile
- ❋ 4 – 3½″ squares of either a colored fabric or photo-transferred pictures*

In our quilt there are pictures of the Colorado state flower, bird, fish, and mammal in each of the corners. You can use more of your center medallion fabric or do something unexpected like photo transfers in these corners.

Puss-in-the-Corner block

Lay out the center medallion and place the 8 multi-triangle units and Puss-in-the-Corner blocks around the medallion, making sure that if you used photos as your center squares they are facing in the right direction. Construct the 4 large corner triangle units (a Puss-in-the-Corner block and 2 multi-triangle units) and then attach to the sides of your center medallion. With the completion of these corners, your square should measure 23¼″ square.

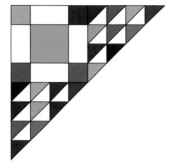

Diagram of large corner triangle unit

BORDER 4

Now it is time to make the center a rectangle. Construct two border units that will go on top of and below the center square you just completed.

For these two borders, you will need:

❋ 6 – 5½″ fussy-cut squares of light toile

❋ 8 half-square triangles, where the short sides measure 6″, to be used as side-setting triangles*

❋ 8 half-squares triangles, where the short sides measure 7″, to be used as corner triangles**

We give you the measurement and numbers needed this way because in our quilt these are very scrappy. If you are doing a more colorful color palette, you will need 2 – 12″ squares cut on each diagonal.

**For a controlled-color quilt you need 4 – 7″ triangles cut in half once on the diagonal for the corner triangles.*

Refer to *Quilter's Academy Vol. 2*, Lesson Two (pages 23–27) for help with measurements on any of these side-setting or corner triangle units. Construct as shown in the following illustration or in Class 590 (page 101).

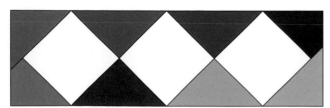

Diagram of triple-square border units

Make your side-setting and corner triangle units a little larger than exact size. If your quilt is not behaving itself in size, you will be able to trim it to be the right size to fit your center medallion square.

To finish this unit, cut the border that lies between the center and the block units you just constructed. For these two interior borders you will need to cut 2 strips of your sashing fabric 1½″ and add it to the top and bottom of the center medallion square. Once sewn, measure from the seamline and trim down to 1¼″, then add the two pieced borders to the top and bottom of the medallion square unit.

BORDER 5

A plain border is next. This is the outer brown border that surrounds the entire center medallion. Here again is a place that if your quilt is not the size you think it should be you can use this border to manipulate the size. Until you get the outer border constructed, you don't know exactly how wide it needs to be. We will help you out a little. Cut 5 – 3″-wide strips. Sew together for length as necessary and then add them to the sides of the center medallion. You can now set this part of your quilt aside for a bit while you construct the outer pieced border unit.

BORDER 6

You will need to construct the 14 – 9″ blocks contained in the border, being extra careful that your blocks all come out to be 9½″. If your blocks are not accurate, completing the construction of your quilt will be difficult.

Once your blocks are constructed, lay them out around your center medallion. Cut the side-setting triangles to create your block border. Refer back to *Quilter's Academy Vol. 2*, Lesson Two (pages 23–27) to pick your favorite method and cut 10 side-setting triangles from the dark toile and 18 side-setting triangles from the light toile.

You will need 14 – 1½″ strips for the sashing. Of these strips, 4 need to remain full length; 3 need to be cut in half so you have 4 – 1½″ × 22″ strips; 5 need to be cut into fourths so you have 20 – 1½″ × 9½″ strips. The last 2 strips need to be cut into 4 – 10½″ lengths and 4 – 11″ lengths. This is easiest to accomplish by cutting two of each size from each strip.

Lay these out between your blocks as shown in the following illustration (sewing 2 strips together where necessary for length). Construct 4 corner units of 2 blocks and 4 light toile side-setting triangles with the sashing between.

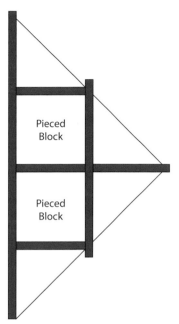

Corner units

Now make the 4 side units. The top and bottom units will have 2 dark toile side-setting triangles and a block. The 2 side units will have 3 dark toile side-setting triangles, 2 blocks, and a single light toile side-setting triangle.

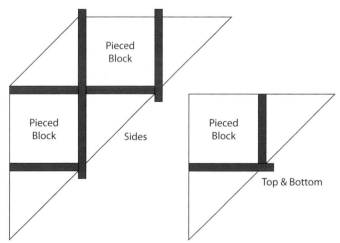

Diagram of side and top and bottom units

Measure the length of these large side units where they will attach to the center medallion unit. This is how large your center medallion needs to measure. Remember we added extra width to the last border on the center medallion, so now you can trim whatever extra width there is away.

Add the 4 side units to the center medallion after you have trimmed the border to size. Add the large corner units you constructed. Be careful to line your sashing pieces up with each other when you do this.

BORDER 7

Our last border was cut 7″ wide and trimmed to 6″ after it was quilted.

Quilt Note: Colorado Memories 2010 was traced onto the quilt before it was quilted and was embroidered during the quilting process in dark brown thread to look like bark.

Class 570

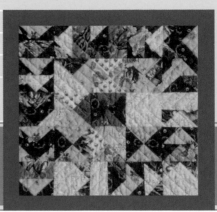

This is one of Harriet's favorite things to do—reproduce antique quilts as accurately and authentically as she can. The two quilts in this chapter are examples of how to work from quilts that are more than 175 years old. They both were hand pieced, hand quilted, and created without the benefit of rotary cutters, electric irons, sewing machines, or excellent light. This is not to degrade these quilts in any way, as we find that we struggle to reproduce them, making very apparent the skills the women of the eighteenth and nineteenth centuries had to create such masterpieces. The sewing machine actually makes our job harder, as we have to be much more precise in our sewing to make everything come out accurately. Hand piecing has more flexibility and small problems can be worked in or out as you come to a bit of a fitting problem. The same could be done with the quilting. Hand quilting gives a lovely soft finish, and small amounts of extra fullness or points that are not perfect get lost in the beautiful stitches. Machine quilting gives a much harder, flatter surface and finish. The machine is no friend to tops that are not perfectly flat and well pieced.

The two quilts in this chapter were chosen for their differences. The first quilt, *Geese in Flight*, is a simple straight-set quilt utilizing many of the techniques taught in *Quilter's Academy Vol. 3*. The sizes of the units are easy to figure out, and would be easy enough to change if you want to change the size or the borders. It is a straightforward project.

The second quilt, *Softly Spoken*, is the total opposite. Because of the Delectable Mountains borders, figuring out the math for the center block is a bit of a job. You will be walked through the drafting process to experience how to work with a quilt that cannot be accurately measured and followed. Not only is the drafting a challenge, but also the piecing needs adjustments as you sew.

So let's start out easy and work our way through *Geese in Flight*.

Geese in Flight

Original antique quilt

Harriet acquired this quilt in a transaction with an antique dealer. It was offered for next to nothing because of the purchase of another quilt in excellent condition. It is badly worn and most of the fabric in the border is worn away, but you can still make out that it was a beautiful pink and brown pillar print. The indigo fabrics are fabulous, and it was one of the few early-nineteenth-century quilts out there for sale with fringe. All the borders fit and turn the corners nicely. The quilting is heavy and a perfect example of how medallion quilts of this era were quilted. The maker of this quilt was obviously quite an accomplished quiltmaker.

The quilt finishes at 86″ square. It is made up of mostly Flying Geese, squares on point, and single dogtooth borders in various sizes. The center is a nine-patch of quarter-square triangle units. Considering the other quilts in this book, this is one of the easier medallions. If you are nervous about your accuracy in working with any of these borders, this is a good starting place, as the sizes are large and easier to work with.

Yardage:

A variety of scraps for center block as well as pieced corner blocks

4 yards cream

4 yards total of various indigo blues

2½ yards border print

Reproduction of original

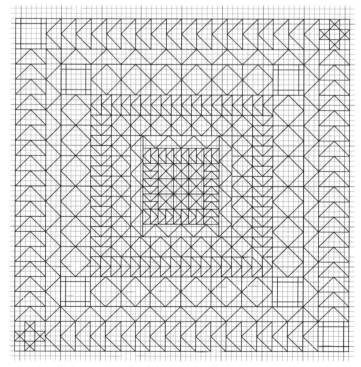

Line drawing of quilt top

Construction

The center block is a collection of different prints sewn into quarter-square triangle units. The units finish 3″ square. You have the option of cutting individual triangles and mixing up the fabrics so that no two are sewn to each other twice, or making the units from squares, which gives you repeats of the same color pairings. If you want a very scrappy look, cut 36 – 4½″ squares from 36 different fabrics. There will be waste, but when you cut the squares into fourths diagonally, the straight grain will be on the long side of the triangle. These can also be cut with a 3″ template (a right triangle with a 3″ hypotenuse) from scraps or strips. Perfect Patchwork Templates Set A, template #4 works perfectly for this. Remember to place the long side of the template on the straight grain.

If you are wanting a more repetitive look, any method of making half-square triangles can be used, then mix them up a bit when sewing the pairs together.

Refer to *Quilter's Academy Vol. 3*, Lesson Two (pages 55 and 56) for detailed instructions for making quarter-square triangles. Once the units are constructed, sew into 3 rows of 3. Be sure that the block measures exactly 9½″. This is important for the fit of the Flying Geese border coming up next.

BORDER 1

This border is 1½″ × 3″ Flying Geese. You will need to construct 32 Flying Geese units, using any technique you choose. The method you choose will be determined by how scrappy you want the geese to be.

The layout of the geese around the center on the original quilt is not symmetrical. The border on the left side of the center is the length of the center, then the bottom border was added, then the right side border, finishing with the top. Play with your geese to see how they look best circling the center block and attach in that order.

Geese layout

Optional layout idea

Once the geese borders are added, the quilt top should measure 15½″, seam allowances included.

BORDER 2

This is a dogtooth border that finishes 2½″ wide, making the length of each triangle 5″. We found that measurement by dividing 3 (the number of triangles along the length of the center square) into 15 (the size of the center square). We strongly recommend that you trim the corners with the Perfect Patchwork Corner Trimmer for this border. Complete instructions are in Class 590 (page 115–117).

You will need to cut:

❋ 14 indigo triangles (4 – 6¼″ squares cut in quarters diagonally)

❋ 16 cream triangles (4 – 6¼″ squares cut in quarters diagonally)

Side borders

The side borders are each made of 3 indigo triangles (outside) and 4 cream triangles (inside). Add a full-sized cream triangle on the ends of the longer border, and square off once attached.

The top and bottom borders are each made of 5 indigo triangles (outside) and 4 cream triangles (inside). The indigo triangles on the ends will be squared off.

Top and bottom borders

Be very careful when attaching borders that the points are accurate and the seams meet to turn the corners cleanly.

Importance of corners

BORDER 3

Diamond-in-a-square border

This is a diamond-in-a-square border. To find the size of the squares needed, measure the size of the quilt top now that Border 2 is attached. If all is going well, it should measure 20½″. The finished size will be 20″, and there are 5 squares on point on the short border. 20″ ÷ 5 = 4″. That is the diagonal measurement of the square. 4″ ÷ 1.414 = 2.82″.

You will need to cut:

❋ 24 – 3⅜″ indigo squares

❋ 14 – 4⅝″ cream squares, cut in fourths diagonally (these could be cut larger for trimming once each border is constructed)

 note *The indigo squares need to finish at exactly 4″ point to point for this border to fit, as well as for the next Flying Geese border to fit. You may have to adjust your seam allowance a bit, as the actual size of the square would be 4″ ÷ 1.414 = 2.82″ + 0.50″ = 3.32″. The closest ruler measure is 0.375″ (⅜″), which is a bit too large. Sew a sample before constructing the complete border to get the square to finish at 4″. We used a full, rather than scant, ¼″ seam allowance for this border.*

Construct two borders using 5 squares and two borders using 7 squares. Keep the white triangles at all the ends full size until they are attached, then trim. This will keep the corners clean and the borders square.

These borders have added a total of 8″ to the size of the center, bringing us up to 28½″, raw edge to raw edge.

BORDER 4

Back to Flying Geese—this time the geese are finished at 2″ × 4″. This makes happy math, as 2 divides evenly into 20. Construct 64 Flying Geese units. Sew 14 geese together for each of the side borders and 18 for the top and bottom borders.

Does your top measure 36½″ on all sides? If so, the rest goes fast, as the sizes keep getting larger.

BORDER 5

Another diamond-in-a-square border is next, this time with the square finishing at 6″ point to point.

You will need to cut:

❋ 24 – 4¾″ indigo squares

❋ 14 – 7¼″ cream squares, cut into quarters diagonally

Construct this border the same as border 3, but this time there is a corner block instead of turning the corner with the border. You will need to make 4 borders using 6 indigo squares in each.

Now we are up to 48½″ raw edge to raw edge.

BORDER 5 CORNER BLOCKS

There are 4 – 6″ corner blocks. The original quilt has Puss-in-the-Corner blocks, but any 6″ block would work if you want to change this. These are very scrappy in the original. We didn't make a traditional Puss-in-the-Corner block where the measurements are shared grid proportions. Our corners are 1″ corners and side strips and a 4″ center square—finished sizes.

Traditional Puss-in-the-Corner block

Adapted Puss-in-the-Corner block

BORDER 6

We are back to another single dog-tooth border, this time having a 6″-long side to the triangle.

You will need to cut:

❋ 8 – 7¼″ indigo squares, cut in quarters diagonally

❋ 9 – 7¼″ cream squares, cut in quarters diagonally

Construct two borders using 8 indigo triangles and 9 cream triangles. Trim the cream triangles after they are attached.

Construct the other two borders using 10 indigo triangles, one on each end of both borders. Half of these will be trimmed away once the borders are attached. This helps us to avoid mitering the corners of this round of borders, or cutting the triangles and creating more seams. This border has added 3″ to each side, bringing us up to 54½″, raw edge to raw edge.

BORDER 7

The final pieced border is 3″ × 6″ Flying Geese units. You will need to construct 72 geese. These are very large geese, and depending on the colors you are working with, you will want to lay out the units around your center to see which way to "fly" the geese for your particular quilt. The direction of the colors can really make a difference in the finished product.

This round of borders uses an Ohio Star block in each of the corners, or any 6″ block of your choice

Ohio Star block

Now that all the pieced borders are attached, the quilt top should be square and measure 66½" on all sides. The addition of the final border, which is 10" wide, brings you to the final measurement of 86".

BORDER 8

Once all the Flying Geese are sewn onto the quilt top, it is time to add the final border. This border can be any width you choose, depending on how large you need it to be or how the border fabric reads on the quilt top. The border on the original is 10" wide.

We hope you have enjoyed the process of making this quilt. Like all medallion quilts, it is a test of accurate sewing and color placement.

Suggested quilting

Softly Spoken

Sortly Spoken posed many more problems than *Geese in Flight*. The *Geese in Flight* medallion is totally a straight setting. There are no angles to contend with and the use of spacers would work if necessary to get the borders to fit if the math got messy. If you are new to medallion quilt-making, it is a good beginner's quilt. *Softly Spoken*, on the other hand, was not so straightforward. Not only is the quilt almost entirely made with triangles, but the center is a square in a square twice over, on point. Any time you start putting squares on point, it is a given that you are going to get into some very messy math—remember the 1.414 equation? Let's walk you through the process of figuring out the grids needed to re-create this beauty.

The quilt dates from the early 1800s, from the Virginia area. The Delectable Mountains border style was very popular in Virginia and North Carolina in the early 1800s, as was the use of stars in the corners of every round of borders. The original quilt also had an applied fringe edge, making it even more elegant.

This quilt was a challenge to draft. The measurements of the center block are very uneven. Things were simply made to fit, and the center block was out of square by almost ½", as you can see in the photo. The quiltmaker did a beautiful job, but because it was hand pieced, she could work with issues as she went. When machine piecing, we are not able to fudge so much.

Close-up of center block and the issues at hand

When Harriet first met this quilt in Pam Kay's bedroom, it took her breath away. The quilting is spectacular, and the fabrics are colorways she had never seen before. She lost sleep for a week dreaming of this quilt and the possibility of making one of her own, just so she could quilt it! Pam graciously sent it home with her to work with. Harriet has yet to meet anyone that has been as excited by this quilt as she was, but wanted to pursue reproducing it. Pam and Harriet challenged themselves to each make one, but Harriet was to do the drafting.

Before going into the details of drafting, let us share with you the dilemma Harriet had with this quilt. The quilting is what took her breath away, and she wanted to reproduce the quilt for the sheer joy of re-creating the quilting. Therefore, the measurements needed to be the same as the original to keep the quilting in the same proportion. That meant that the Delectable Mountains borders needed to be made with 1½″ half-square triangles to get the math to work correctly for the finished width of the solid cream border that the quilting had to fit into. That seemed pretty straightforward, at first. However, the assumption that all the half-square triangles were 1½″ is where the problems started.

Just looking at the center block you can see that the pieces are out of alignment. The half-square triangles appeared to be 1½″, and some of them actually are, so that was the original starting point. The problems started when trying to make a non-square center block fit onto graph paper in a square format. After Harriet drafted the center square to 1½″ half-square triangle measurements, the math was so messy that it would be a nightmare to try to piece. The center square was straightforward, but the half-square triangles for all the Delectable Mountains units would be

a challenge, so back to the drawing board. In the end, this quilt turned out to be the classic solution of working from the outside in. If the solid borders had to be the size that they actually were so the quilting would fit, the first step would be to draft the Delectable Mountains border to the size needed for the solid border. Happily, the 1½″ half-square triangle measure held true. Granted, the corner stars throughout became a bit of a challenge, but doable.

Working in toward the center, the first Delectable Mountains border finishes, point to point, at 19¾″. This makes the first solid border 19¾″ long, including the corner stars.

Now the stars became a consideration, as well as the proportion of the solid border and the width of the quilted feathers. The easiest solution was to make the corner stars 4″ square—a 1″ grid. When the 8″ was subtracted from the 19¾″ measurement (the width of the two borders), Harriet was left with 11¾″. This divided by 8 (the number of units along the edge of the center block) left her with a 1.46″ measurement. This would be okay, very close to 1½″, but the next inner pieced border's edge would be 8″. But 8″ ÷ 6 = 1.333″, a number that most don't want to work with.

By making the border 3⅝″ wide, she was left with a 12½″ center square: 12.5″ ÷ 8 = 1.56″, which is also very close to the 1½″ measure of the Delectable Mountains borders. A 3⅝″ border looked better proportionally. Working backwards, she now had a 12½″ block to break down into units for construction.

To break this down as Harriet did, draw a 12½″ square on a large sheet of eight-to-the-inch graph paper. Tape several small sheets together if you don't have a large sheet. Divide 12.5″ by 8, and you get 1.56″. This translates to 1⁹⁄₁₆″ finished half-square triangles needed for the last row on the center block. Draw a line 1⁹⁄₁₆″ inside the square on all sides. This is the outside pieced border for the center square.

> *note* Before you panic about the ⁹⁄₁₆″ measurement, you will find later on that it is so slight that we don't have to make any compensation for it, as long as you are working with a scant ¼″ seam allowance. The 1½″ half-square triangles work fine; they just don't work out evenly on the graph paper.

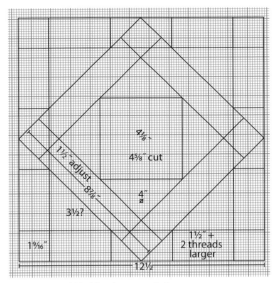

Working in toward the center

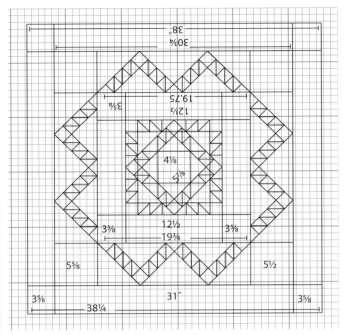

Adding borders out from center

The next triangle border (around the square-in-a-square center) works out to need half-square triangles slightly smaller than 1½". Side to side, this edge finishes at 7⅞". Divide this by 6 to get 1.48". This is close to 1½", but a bit of adjusting will be needed.

On your graph paper, draw in the half-square triangles, making them a tiny bit smaller than 1½". Now you can draw in the square-in-a-square center. The inside edge of the border surrounding the center is 5⅞", making the center square 4⅛" finished.

I understand that this is beyond the patience level of many of today's quilters. But remember, you are in a master's-level book, and we have said all along that precision and accuracy is the key to a wonderful end project, as well as an enjoyable process. By actually doing the drafting, you truly understand what you will need to do to make everything come out okay. The one thing that was consistent was the discrepancy of the corner stars. The large stars were either 5½" or 5⅝" throughout. Be ready to work with these small issues, as you are working with fabric, not paper, and lots of bias and triangles. Be patient with the process.

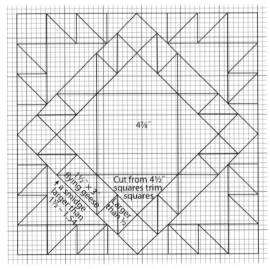

Graph paper drawing

Once you have drafted the block you will know exactly what you will have to adjust during construction. Feel free to go any way you want with the size of this center square. Just keep in mind that the first solid cream border *must be* 19¾" long to fit the Delectable Mountains border. This is non-negotiable.

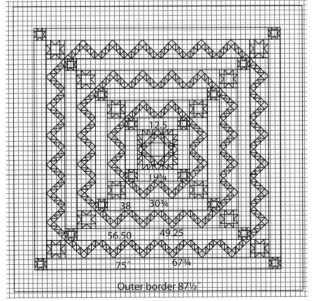

Drawing of entire quilt

tip Here are the finished measurements per border as drafted (page 79).
The slight deviation of ⅛″ has been worked into the final measurements. Your measurements may not be exactly the same, but in order to have all the pieced borders fit, you will need to be extremely close.

Center square: 12½″ finished

Length of first solid border, star to star: 19¾″ finished

Length of first Delectable Mountains border, point to point: 19¾″ finished

Length of first Delectable Mountains border, star to star: 30¾″ finished

Length of second solid border, star to star: 38″ finished

Length of second Delectable Mountains border, star to star: 49¼″ finished

Length of third solid border, star to star: 56½″ finished

Length of third Delectable Mountains border, star to star: 67¾″ finished

Length of fourth solid border, star to star: 75″ finished

Length of outside edge of last pieced border: 87½″

Construction

The yardages listed are general, as I made my version very scrappy, using more than 60 fat quarters of fabrics that gave the look of the original. This quilt lends itself to being very coordinated as well, in which case you will need to figure the yardage for the fabric choices you have made.

For the scrappy version, you will need:

❋ 50–60 different fat quarters of lights, mediums, and darks for the squares, triangles, and half-square triangles in Delectable Mountains units and outside border

❋ 6 or more fat quarters of different indigo blues for stars

❋ 1 yard of a theme fabric (if you are choosing one); In my quilt it is the blue that is in the large Delectable Mountains units.

❋ 2½ yards cream solid

Harriet's Note

It is extremely important *that your seam allowance be not an exact ¼″ measurement but a scant ¼″ (Quilter's Academy Vol. 1, Testing Your Seam Allowance, page 25). You need a seam allowance measurement that gives you* extremely accurate **finished** *pieces. You will be working with ⅛″ increments along the line, and a seam allowance that is too big or small will make it more difficult to achieve the desired results. Sew three half-square units together and iron, then measure the center one. If it does not finish out to the exact size needed, try again by changing your seam allowance size.*

When you make the half-square triangles for this quilt, I suggest that you use the 2½″ Bloc_Loc trimmer. This ruler will snug up tightly to the seam, and has ⅛″ measures around the edges. It makes it much easier to cut the ⅛″ if needed. Because of the issues we encountered in the drafting, it would not be wise to assign given sizes to every piece for the center block. Instead, take it step by step up to the first solid border. At that time the measurements will be static.

Start by cutting a 4⅝″ square for the center of the quilt. Cut 2 – 4″ squares from the next fabric choice and cut each in half diagonally. Sew 2 of these triangles onto opposite sides of the center square, iron, and trim. Check here that the square in between the seams is exactly 4⅛″. If not, this is where you might want to check your seam allowance. Add remaining triangles. Iron and square to exactly 6⅜″. (*Quilter's Academy Vol. 3,* Lesson Three, page 38)

Square-in-a-square center

The first pieced border contains 8 half-square triangles, 4 solid squares, and 4 Flying Geese units (or 8 half-square triangles). The edge that these are to be sewn onto is 5⅞″: 5.875″ ÷ 4 = 1.47″. This is just a hair shy of 1½″. You can either trim the half-square triangles just a couple of threads smaller than 2″ to accommodate this slightly smaller needed size, or try using a foot or needle position that gives you a slightly wider seam. It would be a good idea to make a sample for one side before cutting all of them to be sure they fit. The same consideration needs to be made for the Flying Geese units. Make 4 – 1½″ × 3″ (finished) Flying Geese units.

> **hint** What you need to consider is that 1½″ units joined will be 6″ long for one side, but the square-in-a-square center is 5⅞″. My solution was to sew the units together, changing to the ¼″ foot. The difference between the scant setting and the ¼″ foot was just enough to take in the extra seam to make the units fit exactly. This might be done by moving your needle position over one step as long as it is a very tiny step. Experiment with your machine.

Exact 1½″ half-square triangle makes border too long.

Fits exactly after taking deeper seam

Once the first two sides are attached, join the rest of the half-square triangles for the remaining two sides plus the square corners. Again, make the seam allowance adjustment to make everything fit evenly. The size of the center square should now be 9⅜″, raw edge to raw edge (8⅞″ finished).

CORNERS FOR THE CENTER BLOCK

Construct 8 light blue and 8 dark blue half-square triangle units. Trim them to 2″. Cut 4 cream 2″ squares and 4 – 2½″ dark blue squares. Cut the blue squares in half diagonally. If you are sewing with a scant ¼″ seam allowance, these units should come out exactly to size. Even though the drafting called for 1⁹⁄₁₆″ finished units, the 1½″ units came out perfect on my quilt. If you are concerned about this, you might want to make a sample corner and test it before sewing all the units together. Sew together as shown in the photos below.

Constructing two sides of corner unit

Cut 2 – 4″ squares in half diagonally for the large inner triangle for each corner. Stitch the short side unit onto one side of the triangle. The end single triangle and the larger triangle have been cut larger so that they can be trimmed, eliminating the distortion that so often occurs when working with bias edges.

Attaching first side

Iron the seam allowance toward the large triangle. Attach the second side and iron to the large triangle.

Attaching second side

Once both sides are attached, carefully iron and starch the corners, making sure they are square and flat. Using a ruler, align the ¼″ line up with the triangle points and align the 45° line of the ruler with the outer edge of the corner unit. You will be trimming the large triangle as well as the singles at the ends. Keep everything square and straight with the ruler.

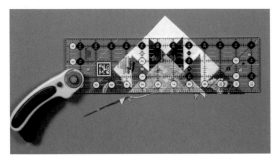
Ruler alignment for trimming

Clean trimmed edge

Attach the corners to the block, making sure that the points on the ends of the single triangles align exactly. If the corner unit is too small, the corners will not turn. If it is too large, you will not get perfect points at the corners.

Perfect fit

The edge-to-edge measurement of the center block should now be 13″ (12½″ finished). If yours is, the rest of the quilt is smooth sailing.

Completed center block

The star in the center of the block was appliquéd. I drafted a 3″ Sawtooth Star on freezer paper, cut along the outside pencil lines and ironed it onto the indigo fabric. A ³⁄₁₆″ seam allowance was cut beyond the cut edge of the paper, and then glued over the freezer paper. I machine appliquéd the star, but hand appliqué would work just as well. A 3″ pieced star could be substituted, framed by strips on all sides, to bring the center up to a finished 4⅛″ square instead of appliquéing the star. The main consideration would be the number of seams in such a small area.

FIRST SOLID BORDER

The first solid border works out to be 3⅝″ wide and 12½″ long. That leaves us needing to make Sawtooth Stars that finish at 3⅝″. Because $3.625″ \div 4 = 0.90″$, these little stars are actually a 9/10″ grid. I made all my units based on a 1″ grid then trimmed very tiny bits off to decrease the size as needed. Make 4 of these little stars for this first border. You will need 16 stars for all 4 solid borders. It might be best to make them all at one time to keep the measurements constant.

Cut 4 – 4¼″ × 13″ long strips of solid fabric for the four borders. Sew the stars onto opposite ends of two of the strips. Attach these borders to the center block.

Once attached, each side needs to measure 20¼″, raw edge to raw edge.

DELECTABLE MOUNTAINS UNITS

These triangle units share a triangle between them, making this a bit different from most Delectable Mountains borders. It also made the drafting a bit more difficult, but the goal was to keep the half-square triangles 1½" for all these blocks.

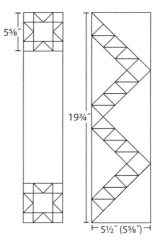

Drafted Delectable Mountains border

First finished Delectable Mountains border

When I started on this project, I went through my stash and pulled every fabric of the era and the look that I wanted to achieve. I found that I was sadly lacking in lights and several colors in values I wanted, so a trip to the store was in order. It took a bit of searching and traveling to find what I needed, but it was a lot of fun to collect the fabrics.

Fabric collection

The constant in the pile is the blue with the pink dots. This was as close as we could get at the time to the blue

in the original quilt. Next, it was time to cut many, many squares from each fabric and start constructing half-square triangles. You are going to need 288 – 2" cut half-square triangles, 48 – 2" squares of light prints, and 60 individual triangles (2½" squares cut in half) of mediums and/or darks to construct the Delectable Mountains units. Because the original quilt was made of whatever was on hand, the blending of colors was wonderful. Harriet followed the color positions in the quilt closely to try to get the same soft look, so extra time and care was taken to pair up the fabric combinations. You can do this border by border or complete them all at one time, then place them as you desire.

To find the size to cut the large triangles, seam allowances were added to the units on the drafted pattern to the left. The short sides of each were measured, and at least ½" was added for trimming to obtain exact edges. The large print triangle is a 6" square cut in half diagonally. You will need to cut 24 squares in half to get 48 triangles. You will also need to cut 18 – 7½" squares of solid cream to get 36 triangles. You will need 12 – 7" squares of solid cream cut in half for the triangles at the ends of the Delectable Mountains borders. These triangles are cut a different size, as we want the straight grain to be on the outside edges of the corners. All these triangles are deliberately cut larger than needed to assure that the long edge can to be trimmed to be exact.

> **note** *These triangles were deliberately cut so that the long edge was on the bias. Because the solid border and star were a given size and cut on the lengthwise grain, I knew there would not be any give in the fabric in case the units were a bit too large or too small. If the long edge of the triangle is on the bias, it can be eased in or stretched a bit for a perfect fit. You will need to pin closely along the entire edge before sewing. Heavy starching once the border is sewn onto the straight-grain border helps everything stabilize and hold its shape.*

Layout of pieces

Starting with the first Delectable Mountains border, lay out the units for the entire border. Start sewing the units together for each mountain. On the left side of the first mountain, sew the single triangle, 3 half-square triangles, and the square together. Iron the seam allowance toward the square, and toward the single triangle. Iron all other seam allowances open. Construct the other side made of 3 half-square triangles. Iron all these seams open. Attach the right side to the triangle first, and iron toward the large triangle. Attach the left side next, ironing again toward the large triangle. This is where you will see that the single triangles and the large triangle are larger that they need to be. This will be taken care of after the complete border is constructed.

Once the mountain units are finished, add the cream triangle to the right edge of the first mountain unit. Iron the seam allowance toward the cream triangle.

Adding cream triangle

Attach the next mountain to the right side of the cream triangle.

Two mountains joined

On the longer borders, continue until all the mountains are joined. Add the corners at both ends.

Corners added to first border

Now it is time to trim the edges to be exactly ¼″ from all the points of the mountains and to square the ends.

Align the ¼″ measure on the edge of your ruler with the points of the mountains. Be sure that the 45° line on the ruler is aligned with one of the triangle seams to assure accuracy.

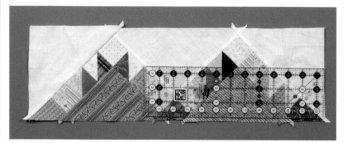
Aligning ruler for trimming

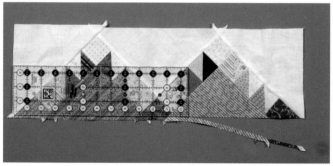
Continue the length of the border

Turn the border around to trim the other side. The border, after trimming, should measure exactly 6″. If you have sewn and ironed well, this will be what you have. If not, you will need to go back and find the problem, as nothing will fit from here on in if the borders are not to size. Using a wide or square ruler, align the 6″ measure with the trimmed side, at the same time aligning the ¼″ measure exactly on the points of the triangles, again using the 45° line on the ruler to keep everything straight and square.

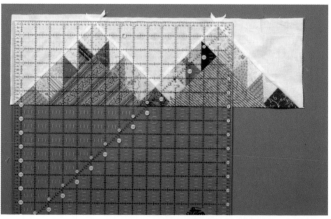
Trimming to exactly 6″

Trim the corners to be square with the sides. Measure the length of the first border. It needs to be exactly 20¼″ (19¾″ finished).

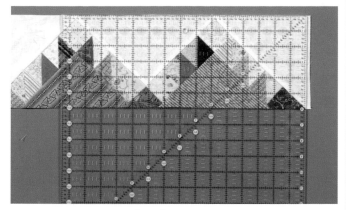

Squaring corners

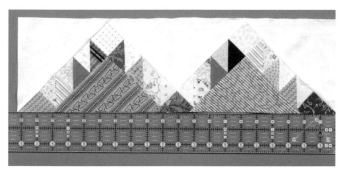

Exact length achieved

The stars at the end of each pieced border are the size that the border is wide. The Delectable Mountains units finished at 5½″, cut 6″. That results in a grid of 1⅜″. This is much easier than the little stars, as ⅛″ measurements are on our rulers! You will need 12 of these stars.

OUTSIDE BORDER

This hourglass border contains squares, triangles, and pieced triangles.

Cut:

❊ 48 – 4⅞″ squares of cream

❊ 52 – 2⅝″ squares of various colors

❊ 52 – 3″ squares, cut in half diagonally, of various colors

❊ 8 – 2⅞″ × 4⅝″ rectangles cream solid for corners

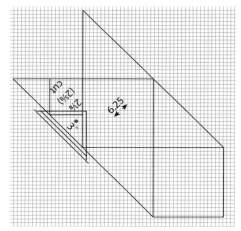

Drafted pattern for border

Border layout

Start building the borders by making the pieced triangles.

Pieced triangles

75¼

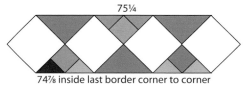

74⅞ inside last border corner to corner

Connecting squares and pieced triangles

Lay out all the units to place colors to your liking. Sew units together as shown in photo.

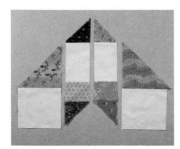

Pieced corner

In order to turn the corner, you will need to work with half-squares of the cream solid. This is where the rectangles in the cutting list are used. Join a small triangle, a small square, and a rectangle end to end. Attach these units to both ends of all four borders.

Attach this border to your quilt top, mitering the corners. Once all the borders are sewn on, add the last two small triangles to each corner. These can be added to the rectangles in the above step, if desired.

Congratulations! You now have a fantastic quilt top to show for all your efforts. We hope you really put your heart into the quilting so that in 190 years someone will discover your quilt and lose sleep dreaming about it.

Class 580

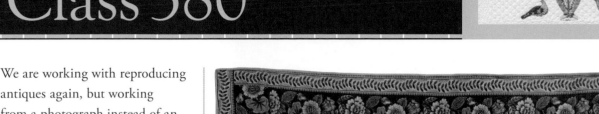

We are working with reproducing antiques again, but working from a photograph instead of an actual quilt. This becomes more like making a representation of a quilt, as there is a lot of guessing in figuring out sizes and making needed changes to make things fit together.

The two quilts in this chapter are both antique quilts owned by museums, so not readily available to everyone to actually look at up close and take measurements. What you have to start with is the image and generally a size—length and width. Even this information is dicey, as the quilts are very old, generally used and worn, and shrinkage and distortion have taken place over the years. If the quilt is hanging instead of lying flat when photographed, or the photo is not of high quality, the problems just keep adding up.

The *Variable Star and Nine-Patch Medallion* is also named the *Hewson-Center Quilt with Multiple Borders* by the American Folk Art Museum, where it is currently living.

Hewson-Center Quilt with Multiple Borders, artist unidentified; center block printed by John Hewson (1744–1821), United States, 1790–1810; cotton and possibly linen; 85½″ × 76″; Collection American Folk Art Museum, New York, Gift of Jerry and Susan Lauren, 2006.5.1.

Photo by Gavin Ashworth

First reproduction of the quilt

The panel in the center is a John Hewson panel. It was block printed, and when you find this panel in various antique quilts, you find that the panel was printed in several configurations. This means that there was no set size for the panel. The original quilt measures 76″ × 85½″. Because there is no documentation for the size of the panel, working from the outside in makes the most sense.

We started by taking off the border allotment. Looking at the quilt, we guesstimated it to be about 9″ wide. That takes off 18″ from the length and width, leaving 58″ × 67½″. The quilt has 11 blocks across and 13 blocks down the side. Dividing 11 into 58″ gives a block size of 5.27″. Dividing 67½″ by 13 gives 5.19″. So far we are looking at a block size of 5.25″. The next decision is if this works with the two different blocks. The star block is a three-patch, so 5.25″ ÷ 3 = 1.75″, or a 1¾″ grid. Nice math! The Puss-in-the-Corner block is technically a four-patch block, so 5.25″ ÷ 4 = 1.31″—not nice math. However, there is no reason that the center rectangle can't be a different size combined than the corners. So if the corners are 1¼″, that leaves 2¾″ for the center. It will still look like a Puss-in-the-Corner block, just with the center unit not a true combined grid size, which technically should be 2½″. This is an easy solution.

Now let's look at the size of the center. The center panel plus the dogtooth borders equals 7 blocks, and 7 × 5.25″ = 36.75″. There are five triangles in the dogtooth border that are next to the blocks; 36.75″ ÷ 5 = 7.35″, or about 7⅜″ long. If these triangles are cut on the bias, fitting in the extra bit would not be difficult.

To find the width of the dogtooth border:

7.375″ ÷ 2 = 3.69″, or just shy of 3¾″ wide

If you subtract the 7½″ for the two dogtooth borders, you are left with a 29½″ center panel.

Depending on what you choose to use for the center panel, this might be large, or too small. So back to the drawing board. The first hurdle is to find a measurement that can be divided by 3 into ruler-happy numbers for the Variable Star block. The Puss-in-the-Corner block is very adaptable. Working back into the center, you will be able to adjust sizes to your needs.

The first quilt we made from this photo is shown above with the appliqué center panel. Carrie spent hours cutting out flowers, vines, and leaves, and placing them to create an old-looking piece of fabric. Broderie Perse techniques were used for the appliqué. This center panel could be adjusted in size to fit whatever measurements were needed.

Variable Star and Nine-Patch Medallion

Second version of the quilt

The second quilt was made when the John Hewson panel was printed and made available. A new problem emerged when the measurements of the panel turned out to be 21″ × 23½″, and the birds on the sides at the top and bottom of the panel were missing. To get the panel to a workable size, strips of background fabric had to be added and the birds and butterflies Broderie Perse appliquéd to the background. By having to do this, we could cut the center panel to finish at 30″, keeping the center the same size as we figured on the previous page.

Reproduction of center panel

This quilt is easy to piece and put together, so playing with the math is worth the time. Start with your center design or panel, and go from there. Remember, the photos can be just inspiration to get you started or the basis of a close reproduction. You are the quiltmaker.

Finished quilt: 76″ × 85″

We are not giving yardages for this quilt as there are too many variables based on your personal size decisions. The original is a very scrappy quilt, so putting a palette of fabrics together will be determined by the final look you are going for.

Blocks needed for quilt

Fabric group that made the color palette for the printed panel

Construction

You will need to construct:

❋ 4 dogtooth borders using 16 dark triangles and 12 light triangles; Use 8⅝″ squares cut into quarters diagonally (for straight-grain edges) or 6″ squares cut in half diagonally (for bias on edges) to obtain these triangles.

❋ 4 corner triangles—cut 2 – 8½″ squares, and cut in half diagonally (oversized)

❋ 16 – 5½″ (finished) Ohio Star blocks

❋ 30 – 5½″ (finished) Puss-in-the-Corner blocks

❋ 48 – 5½″ squares cut from various fabrics

The construction of this quilt top is basic and straight-forward. Everything you need to know you have learned in *Quilter's Academy Vol. 1–3*. We feel it would be redundant to rewrite all the directions for these simple blocks when we have already done it in previous books. Once you get the center size determined, do the math and run with it.

The Ohio Star blocks are quarter-square triangles and squares. Instructions for making quarter-square triangles are found in *Quilter's Academy Vol. 3*, Lesson Two (page 55).

The Puss-in-the-Corner blocks are a combined-grid block, which we discussed in *Quilter's Academy Vol. 1*, Class 170 (page 83).

Instructions for the dogtooth border can be found in Class 590 (page 115). The formula will need to be worked using the size of the center square you decide to use for your personal quilt to determine the size of the triangles.

This quilt is a perfect candidate for a center photograph, embroidery, or large panel that is readily available in quilt stores. It would look just as good in wild colors as the subdued ones of yesteryear. Have fun getting creative with this one.

The Virginia Framed Medallion

Harriet's version of *The Virginia Framed Medallion* (pictured on page 16)

This is a truc framed medallion. A series of heavily pieced borders is all that is involved and produces a stunning display of various piecing techniques all playing well with each other. This quilt can be quite a challenge, as there are no plain strips added between the pieced borders. This can make the math for some of the borders tricky to say the least.

The inspiration for making this quilt was a photo of it in the Virginia Quilt Museum catalog. Harriet was drawn to the quilt when Quilting Treasures did a line of fabrics based on this quilt in 2007. The company did a free pattern but it was a simplified version of the original, and the fabrics used were limited to the line. She has been collecting fabrics since then, keeping them in a box until the time arose to make the quilt. This is finally the time.

The original quilt measures 88″ × 99″. When Harriet started working out the size of the borders on graph paper, she found that the sizes of many of them were not ruler- or sewing machine–friendly. To make the borders standard sizes, the quilt would finish at 88″ × 100″. This size would start with a 9″ center star, which she felt was too large and heavy. She wanted a smaller quilt, so she started with a 6″ star. If you draft your own version, you could start with any size that is divisible by 4 for the star, then work out from there to see what size each of the borders would need to be. Eventually, you will run into a math problem with this quilt, regardless of what size center you start with.

We are going to give you the measurements Harriet used to create the new quilt, as well as the ways she got around some of the size issues. Some of the methods are a bit unorthodox, but that is the joy of truly knowing how to work with fabric and knowing what you can get away with. This is in no way promoting sloppy workmanship; in fact, it was done to achieve perfect points and accuracy within the piecing itself. Harriet did not want to chop off points or add spacers unless absolutely necessary, so other techniques were utilized.

We want to strongly point out that the measurements given work on the machine we are sewing on, along with our ironing techniques and so on. As we have been teaching throughout this series, you have to be accurate within your own workmanship skills. We do not guarantee that these measurements will give you the same results; therefore, we strongly suggest that you draft the quilt out and discover the measurements for yourself. You can choose to start with a different size star and follow along with the techniques, but figure your own sizes and measurements using the formulas given. You can change the size of any one border and then go off on your own, or even change the design or size of one or more borders. By this point in the series, it is our hope that you would be able to come up with the solutions you will find you need.

> *note* *The secret to this quilt, as well as everything we have taught in this series, is that the seam allowance is not important, but the finished measurement of the unit is critical!*
>
> *If you expect your piecing to match your drafting, you will have to pay close attention to your cutting, sewing, and ironing to obtain perfect-measure finished units. If you are still struggling with this, go back to Quilter's Academy Vol. 1, Class 110 (page 5) and Class 120 (page 12) and get it right before you start. This goes for all the quilts in this book.*

Construction

CENTER STAR

Center Star layout

This is a 6″ star, made in a 1½″ grid. The center of the star is a square-in-a-square (*Volume 3*, Class 330, page 38). Cut the center square 2⅝″ and the side triangles 2⅞″ to get a 3″ finished square-in-a-square. The Flying Geese units on the sides are 1½″ × 3″ finished, and the corner squares are 1½″ finished. Use whatever techniques you prefer to make the elements for this block.

BORDER 1—PLAIN STRIP

This little border is ½″ finished. Cut your strips an extra ⅛″ wide so that once sewn onto the star, the strips can be trimmed to exactly ¾″.

BORDER 2— SMALL SAWTOOTH BORDER

Sawtooth border

This sawtooth border is made of 1″ finished half-square triangles. You will need to construct 32. We used two different fabrics for the half-square triangles, a red and a brown.

BORDER 3—PLAIN STRIP

Another plain border, this one finishes at 1¼″. Cut the strips 1⅞″ wide, attach, and trim to be exactly 1½″ wide. The center should now measure 11½″, or 12″ raw edge to raw edge.

BORDER 4—DIAMOND-IN-A-SQUARE

Diamond-in-a-square border

This is a square on-point border, so now diagonal measurements come into play. There are half-squares at the ends of each border, utilizing a larger half-square triangle to turn the corner. You could use anything else you want to put in the corners; the original quilt used small Sawtooth Stars.

The size of the piece is now 11½" square, finished. You will need to divide this number to see how many units you can get in this space evenly. If you divide 11.5" by 6, you get 1.91", or 1⅞"; 1.875" ÷ 1.414 = 1.32", or about 1⅜". Because the math is messy and not spot on, we suggest that you cut the side triangles so the bias is the long edge. The bias edge allows the edge to stretch, or be eased in, for any slight problem that may need to be accommodated as the borders are attached. When the finished border was measured, the triangles were a hair longer that the squares, point to point. By manipulating the fabric in this way, you can work with numbers that are not exact.

Cut the squares 1⅞" square. The side triangles were cut from 2½" squares, cut in half diagonally. These triangles are oversized to allow for trimming to obtain a straight edge, exactly ¼" from the points.

Add an extra square on each end of each border, then trim to allow for seam allowances. Add another half-square triangle or star in each corner. This border finished at 1⅞", so the quilt is now 15⅜" + ½" seam allowances or 15⅞".

> *note* You might start to find that your measurements do not match those listed. This is where the principles of medallions really come into play. You will need to change seam allowances, redraft to a different size, or add coping strips here and there to keep the math the same. All of these options are at your disposal. Try to make this a creative adventure instead of a frustrating situation. A good challenge is good for the mind!

BORDER 5— DOUBLE SAWTOOTH BORDER

Double sawtooth border

This border is a double sawtooth. It creates real movement to the quilt at this point.

Because the next border is Flying Geese that need to fit evenly, this border needs to be 2½" wide. This is a very easy border to make any size, as it is made of rectangles with flipped corners to create the triangles.

Cut 60 – 1½" × 3" rectangles from background fabric. Cut 120 – 1½" squares of the fabric you want for your points.

Draw a diagonal line from corner to corner on the wrong side of each of the squares.

Place a square on one end of each of the rectangles and stitch on the line.

Sewing first square

Iron the square toward the corner, making sure the edges line up. Trim the seam allowance ¼" beyond the stitching.

Repeat the process for the opposite end of each rectangle, making sure the seam is going the same direction as the first. Iron and trim.

Second side

Lay out 15 rectangles and stitch them together to make the border. Repeat this four times.

Again, choose what block you want in the corners, then attach the borders to the top.

These borders have added 5" to the top, which should now measure 20⅜" plus seam allowances.

BORDER 6— SMALL FLYING GEESE BORDER

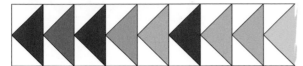

Small Flying Geese border

This border is straightforward—a simple border of 1½″ × 3″ Flying Geese. These are a great place to really mix up the fabrics and make a very scrappy border. You will need to make 56 Flying Geese units, using any method of your choice.

These borders add 6″ to the size, so we are now up to 26½″ plus seam allowance. Remember, this is mathematically correct. You may be off by ⅛″ or so as you go, but this is workable by easing and light stretching if necessary.

How are you doing?

BORDER 7—HOURGLASS BORDER

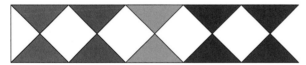

Hourglass border

We're back to squares on point again. They now have to fit into 26½″. The diagonal measurement of the squares is 26.5″ ÷ 9 = 2.94″, or 3″.

After making a trial sample, we found the closest measurement that would work was to cut the squares 2⅝″ square. The side triangles are 3″ squares cut in half diagonally. This again gives bias edges to work with on the edges for fitting assistance.

Cut 40 – 2⅝″ squares of background fabric.

Cut 36 – 3″ squares from a variety of fabrics, then cut in half diagonally.

Add a full square at each end of each border, and then trim once the units are sewn together. This border finishes at 2⅞″ wide.

Quilt Note: As the borders get longer, it is a good idea to size them on the ironing board before you try to attach them to the quilt top. This border needs to be 27″ long, raw edge to raw edge. Measure 27″ on your ironing board and use a pin or a line to mark 27″. Lay the border on the

ironing board and see if it fits this length. If it is too short by a bit, spray with starch, lightly stretch, and iron with a dry iron until the new size is set. If it is a bit too long, spray with starch and gently use your hand to ease in the fullness evenly and shrink by slowly lowering the iron down onto the fabric, giving it time to pull in a bit and "shrink." Do this after you have trimmed the edges.

Add this border to the four sides, using blocks of your choice in the corners.

BORDER 8— LARGE SAWTOOTH BORDER

Large sawtooth border

We are back to an easy border made of half-square triangles. The size of the top is now 32½″. We can add 13 – 2½″ half-square triangles evenly—32.5″ ÷ 13 = 2.5″.

Construct 52 – 2½″ (finished) half-square triangles using your background and 1 fabric. Add a corner block of your choice.

Our quilt top is now 37½″ square.

BORDER 9— SAWTOOTH STAR BORDER

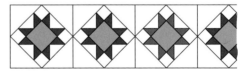

Sawtooth Star border

The next border is made of Sawtooth Star blocks on point. It is going to take a bit to figure out the size needed for the star blocks. To find the number of stars needed, we need to divide 37.5″ by how many stars we think might fit in without getting too large or too small.

Start by dividing 37.5″ by 8 to get a diagonal measurement of 4.6″, a bit larger than 4⅝″. This sounds good so far. The size of the square (4.625″ ÷ 1.414) is 3.27″, or about 3¼″. Next, 3.25″ ÷ 4 = 0.81″, or a ¹³⁄₁₆″ grid for the star. Now the measurements are getting messy.

Change the size of the stars to a ¾″ grid. That makes a 3″ block. The diagonal measurement of a 3″ block is 4.24″, and 8 of these equals 33.93″. You need a length of

35.36″—about 1½″ short. Each star needs to be ¼″ larger point to point. The math looks like this:

4.24″ + 0.25 = 4.49″ ÷ 1.414 = 3.12″. That is 3¹⁄₁₀″ and definitely not ruler-friendly.

If the stars are made with a ⅞″ grid, the stars are 3½″, and 3.5″ × 1.414 = 4.95″ × 8 = 39.59″. Now they are 2″ too long.

Because of the size dilemma, we ended up making a test border of 8 stars using ¾″ × 1½″ (cut 1¼″ × 2″) Flying Geese, corner squares cut 1¼″, and the center squares 2″. These stars finished at 3″. The border finished to be about 1¾″ too short.

Back to the drawing board. Another 8 stars were made cutting the Flying Geese units ¹⁄₁₆″ larger, the corner squares 1⅝″ and the center square 2⅛″, making the overall block ¼″ larger, thinking this would solve the problem. Math on a calculator and actual fabric are far from the same thing in reality.

The second stars finished at 3⅜″. The diagonal measurement was 4¾″. This border finished 2″ too long.

Mathematically, this should not have happened. By adding the extra ¼″, you would have thought that things would have been within ½″ or less. But … once it was all said and done, the stars didn't need to be ¼″ larger; instead, the diagonal measurement needed to be ¼″ larger. So we're back to where we started—ugly math and measurements that just don't work with fabric.

The solution for this problem came down to adding spacers at the end of each row, or making larger stars, which would be out of proportion with the other borders. We opted to use the 3″ stars, adding ½″ spacers at the end of each row, and placing another 3″ star in the corners. The spacers are hardly noticed and the proportion of the stars is in keeping with the other borders. (See the Class 520 closeup, page 26.)

> *tip* There are times when just a thread or two can make all the difference in the size of the unit needed. This is not something a ruler and rotary cutter can do for you. Harriet found that just changing the seam allowance was all it took to make things fit perfectly. She almost always pieces with a scant ¼″ seam allowance. However, when the units are just a few threads too large, she changes to her ¼″ foot. This takes up just enough extra that the blocks shrink up to be a perfect size with an unfriendly ruler measurement in the end. It is worth a try when the fractions are causing problems.

If you run across this problem in any border that is working with bias and diagonal-set blocks, there is a solution to working with sizing issues if they are within ½″ or less by using the bias to your advantage. This sounds unorthodox, but using starch and heat, you are able to gently stretch the bias stars and edges to just the right length without having them look distorted. This is a very unusual treatment for fabric, but desperation is the mother of invention. Once the quilt is quilted, the slight stretch will not cause a problem.

If you get a chance to study antique medallion quilts, you will find very odd solutions to these types of problems. Borders are cut off at any point just to make them fit, points of blocks are lopped off to get the size needed, various size units are used within a border to make things fit, and so on. You get the idea … they did what they had to in order to keep things going. Think of this as the most fun element about these quilts. You get to be inventive and creative in finding solutions for the problems that crop up.

The quilt top is now 45½″ square (46″ raw edge to raw edge).

BORDER 10— LARGE FLYING GEESE BORDER

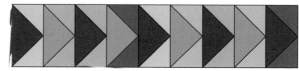

Large Flying Geese border

The tenth border brings us back to Flying Geese. Fortunately the size of the quilt top after adding the 3″ Sawtooth Star border brought us to a size that can accommodate 2″ × 4″ Flying Geese, with a bit of fitting when attaching the Flying Geese borders. Geese are a bit stretchy, so when they are attached to each other into the border, pull on them slightly after starching to extend the border by the ½″ needed. Over a 45″ span, ½″ is such a small measurement that it won't be at all noticeable that the size was adjusted, but you will get a perfect fit.

You will need to make 100 geese units, 23 each for the top and bottom edges and 27 each for the sides. These are very scrappy.

Our quilt top is now approximately 54″ square.

BORDER 11—PINWHEEL BORDER

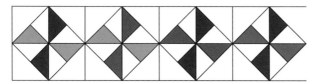

Pinwheel border

This border appears only on the top and bottom of the quilt top. The Pinwheel blocks are another on-point block, as the Sawtooth Star blocks were. Looking at the photo of the original, you will see that there are 10 Pinwheel blocks and half of a pinwheel at one end of each border. Because we changed the scale of the quilt to be smaller, it worked out that the half-block was not needed.

To figure the size of the Pinwheels, the process is the same as for the Sawtooth Stars.

The length of the edge these will be attached to is now 54″. To keep the Pinwheel block from getting too large, we divided 11 blocks into 54″.

> 54″ ÷ 11 = 4.90″
> This is the diagonal measurement for the block we need.

> 4.90″ ÷ 1.414 = 3.47″
> This gives us a 3½″ block.

Double check the math:

> 3.5″ (block size) × 1.414 = 4.95″ (diagonal of block) × 11 = 54.44″ border

We know that the diagonal set gives us side-setting triangles along the sides so we will be able to manipulate the fabric to stretch or ease slightly to get a good fit.

You need 22 Pinwheel blocks. The finished size of the half-square triangles is 1¾″, cut 2¼″. They can be turned different directions for interest.

Layout for Pinwheel blocks

BORDER 12—
SMALL SAWTOOTH BORDER

Small Sawtooth border

Finally, a simple border! This little border of half-square triangles is on all sides of the quilt top, containing the inner borders very nicely. Our quilt top is now at 54″ × 64″. These measurements allow us to use 1¼″ half-square triangles on all sides, knowing that there will need to be a slight bit of fitting involved when attaching the borders.

Measure all sides of your quilt top and find the size half-square triangles you need to fit. We used 1¼″ half-square triangles.

Join enough squares to match the length of the top. Attach both borders to the sides of the quilt top.

When joining the squares for the top and bottom borders, turn the last one on each end as shown below.

Turning corners

BORDER 14—
STREAK OF LIGHTNING BORDER

Streak of Lightning border

The final border is called Streak of Lightning. It is made of 1″ strips separating scrappy triangles. The quilt now measures 56½″ × 66½″.

Because this border is on the outside edge, we need to make sure that the grainline is straight with the long sides of the triangles.

To find the size of the triangles, you will need to find a number that divides evenly into the measurements of the quilt top.

$$56.5'' \div 11 = 5.13''$$

$$66.5'' \div 13 = 5.11''$$

Things are looking good. On the original, the borders ended wherever they may and were cut off where they ended. We want the corners to turn in a nice straight line, so we need to have measurements that match each other for each side of the quilt.

The long side of each triangle needs to finish at 5⅛" to fit well. Because the long side of the triangles is on the straight grain, we no longer have the option of easing or stretching to make them fit. To find the size square the triangles will be cut from, we recommend that you use graph paper instead of calculator measurements. That way if your size requirements don't end with happy ruler numbers, you have a template to cut from.

Draw a triangle, having the long side be the measurement you need. Add seam allowances to all sides and measure point to point of the seam allowance to get the size square that will be cut twice diagonally.

Our formula looks like this:

$$5.125'' + 0.625'' + 0.625'' = 6.37'' \text{ or } 6⅜''$$
The 0.625" is the seam allowance extension of the points. Refer to *Quilter's Academy Vol. 3*, Class 350 (page 66) for more information.

We recommend that you cut these squares larger, as we know that triangles in this position do not always hold true to their needed finished size once sewn, and the extra allows for trimming so that the points of the white strip are exactly at the seamline.

The "streak" is a finished 1" strip. Refer to Class 590 (page 125) for instructions on constructing this border. The units are shown below.

Adding lightning strip to mirrored triangles

Our version of *The Virginia Framed Medallion* finished at 58" × 72". If you are interested in making this a bed-sized quilt instead, we have made a list of measurements for you to work with that are more accurate to the original quilt. *These are suggested measurements*, and we recommend that you draft out the quilt using these measurements and make sure you like the scale and the size of each border. As you know, rounding up and down on a calculator can make a measurable difference in finished size, and the following measurements are just calculator measurements. You will still need to work out the details for yourself. This is just a jumping off point to get you started.

The following measurements are for a quilt about 88" × 100":

Center star: 9½" finished

Border 1: ½"-wide strip, finished

Border 2: 1½" half-square triangles

Border 3: 2¼"-wide strip, finished

Border 4: 3"-wide finished diamond-in-a-square border (if you want stars in the corners as in the original, the star is a ¾" grid).

Border 5: 3½"-wide double sawtooth border, finished (⅞" grid stars for corners)

Border 6: 4½"-wide Flying Geese border finished (1⅛" grid stars for corners)

Border 7: 4"-wide hourglass border, finished (1" grid star for corners)

Border 8: 3" half-square triangles, finished (¾" grid stars for corners)

Border 9: 4+" stars – 5¾"-wide Variable Star border

(You will run into the same problem with this size as we did on the smaller version. The 4" stars need to be a tiny bit larger than 4" to come out evenly. Refer back to how we handled this problem.)

Border 10: 5"-wide Flying Geese border

Border 11: About 6¼" wide. Pinwheels are made from 2¼" half-square triangles.

Border 12: 1½" half-square triangles

Border 13 (final): 4½"-wide Streak of Lightning border— corners don't turn but end like original quilt.

BORDER DESIGNS AND TECHNIQUES

Class 590

We have attempted to create an invaluable reference work for the many borders that are used in traditional medallion quilts, as well as different techniques for creating them. Each page will have an illustration and photo of the border design, and the different ways you might want or need to piece them. We chose to do this so that the borders would be more adaptable to your designing process. When strip piecing and rotary cutting are the only options, several borders would have to be eliminated because of the math and measurement problems the various sizes of borders require. When templates are an option, any size can be made with a bit of drafting, a good drafting ruler, and a calculator. We certainly hope you have been working through the drafting techniques as you've progressed through the first four volumes of *Quilter's Academy* and this is not coming at you as new information. Drafting allows you to make many design decisions that you won't find in books or patterns. This is not about speed, but about design and precision.

You will also find that many of the borders are wonderful when the same fabrics are repeated over and over, but the same design adds a lot to the quilt if the pieces are scrappy. Strip techniques limit the scrappy look, but template cutting opens endless possibilities. Keep an open mind and don't look at the clock. It is all about the finished product, but in order to enjoy the work to be done, you need to enjoy the process and appreciate the progress, instead of racing to the end and not enjoying the journey.

There are many more borders that we have not covered that have a more contemporary look. You might want to add them to the quilts you design. One of our favorite

sources is an older book by Jinny Beyer, *The Art and Technique of Creating Medallion Quilts*. This book was released in 1982 and was responsible for the resurgence of interest in medallion quilts. With the use of the Jinny Beyer fabric lines and border prints, fantastic original quilts were very popular in the 1980s and into the 1990s. You might get hooked on these challenging quilts! You will also find that you can design your own original borders. We have not tried to cover every aspect of borders, just the tried and true ones that occur regularly in traditional medallion quilts. They can be used on any other quilt also. The possibilities are endless; only your imagination will slow you down.

The borders will be grouped by type: squares, rectangles, triangles, zigzags, and so on. The illustrations will show the process of making the borders, but individual techniques for making the necessary units will not be included, as we have covered that extensively in previous books. We may make a notation of which *Quilter's Academy* volume the technique can be found in. As we always preach, precision and attention to detail can't be stressed here enough. Borders need to fit correctly in length, and stay accurate in width throughout the entire length of the border. We will also give you any math formulas you might need for resizing borders. Proportions are important, and often a spacer needs to be inserted to keep the sizing and fit correct.

Because we are working in decimal point measurements and you will need to be rounding up and down, keep this chart handy for assistance in finding the next best number to work with.

DECIMALS TO INCHES

Once you have calculated the size of your borders, use this chart to determine if you need to enlarge your quilt top by the addition of small strip borders. Whether you round up or down is up to you. If the answers are minute, you will most likely be able to ease in the tiny bit of extra or gently stretch a tiny amount in to fit. If either of these solutions would cause distortion, you will need to go back and rethink adding that extra strip. The longer the distance to fit, the more likely you would be to round up. The smaller the edge to fit, the more likely you would round down.

Decimal to fraction	Rounded to nearest ¼″
0 to 0.12″	0
0.13″ to 0.37″	¼″ (0.25″)
0.38″ to 0.62″	½″ (0.5″)
0.63″ to 0.87″	¾″ (0.75″)
0.88″ to 0.99″	1″

Decimal to fraction	Rounded to nearest ⅛″
0 to 0.6″	0
0.07″ to 0.18″	⅛″ (0.125″)
0.19″ to 0.31″	¼″ (0.25″)
0.32″ to 0.43″	⅜″ (0.375″)
0.44″ to 0.56″	½″ (0.5″)
0.57″ to 0.68″	⅝″ (0.625″)
0.69″ to 0.81″	¾″ (0.75″)
0.82″ to 0.93″	⅞″ (0.875″)
0.94″ to 0.99″	1″

Squares and Rectangles

The simplest borders are made from straight-set squares and rectangles. The piecing is straightforward and the math is easy to figure out what size unit is needed to fit the edge of the quilt top. Below is a variety of straight borders for you to consider.

PIANO KEYS BORDER

Piano Keys border

Piano Keys is one of the easiest pieced borders to make. They have been used extensively over many years as a way to use up small scraps within a border. Illustrated below is a repeat of six colors. A band of strips is sewn together (see note) then cut into the width you want your border to be, then sewn together end to end to the length you need.

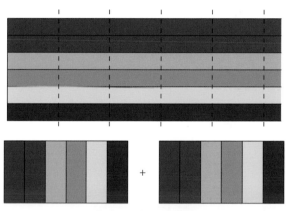

Construction process

> *note* Don't forget all you have learned about accuracy. In order for the borders to fit, each finished unit needs to be the exact measurement. This is achieved by cutting and sewing accurately, but even more important is ironing and starching correctly, trimming each strip as it is added, and measuring the final unit to check for the correct measurement. Reread Quilter's Academy Vol. 1, Class 120 (page 12) and Class 130 (pages 12–28), for a refresher.

You can alternate just two colors for a true piano key look.

For a contemporary look, try shading the colors from light to dark.

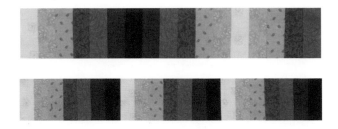

You can mix up the widths of the strips with random measurements.

Even more exciting is creating a scrappy look. Instead of the bands from the same color repeats, use random colors and shorter strips to get the most variety.

This border is very easy to make fit any edge. You can change the width of the strip and the width of the border very easily. Not a lot of math or fitting involved.

As for corner treatment, you can run the strips off the edge, which was very common on antique quilts, use a plain square in the corner, miter the corner, add a fussy-cut fabric motif, or any of a myriad of ideas. This border is very versatile.

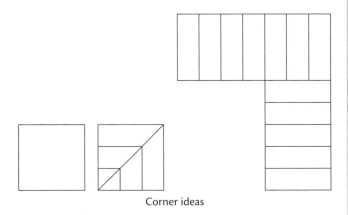

Corner ideas

CHECKERBOARD (OR FOUR-PATCH) BORDER

Similar to Piano Keys, checkerboards can come in many variations. This is a very graphic border if the fabrics are high in contrast, but can also be very subtle with close-value color choices. These borders are made of alternating squares, generally of just two fabrics. For a scrappy look, use a variety of fabrics.

Checkerboard border

Scrappy checkerboard border

Constructing this border is the same as making four-patches. We suggest that you fan the seams (*Quilter's Academy Vol. 1*, Class 150, page 58) to eliminate bulk and distortion when ironing.

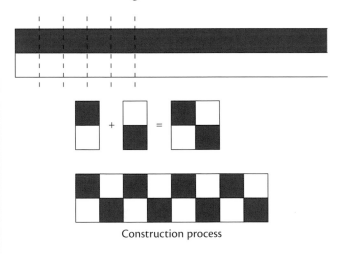

Construction process

Below are a number of different ways to work with squares in borders.

Different spacer sizes

RECTANGLES

Following through with the ideas of using squares, let's add rectangles into the mix, but still working with the idea of repeats and a checkerboard look.

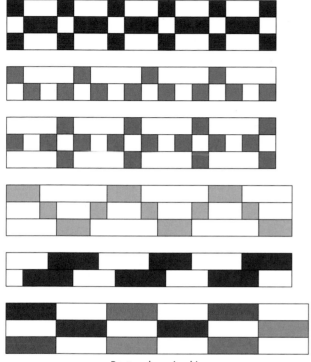

Rectangles mixed in

Checkerboard Blocks

Incorporating pieced checkerboard blocks into a border is another way to give a lot of graphic impact with simple piecing and math. Below are three ideas to try. These would be most effective in a small grid of 1″ or less.

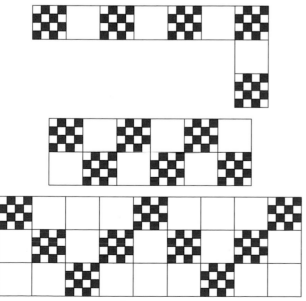

Using checkerboard blocks

SQUARES AND RECTANGLES ON POINT

Two colorways for squares on point

Now the borders start to get more interesting and exciting to work with, but the math becomes tricky. Remember the 1.414 formula for measuring squares on point? If not, go back to *Quilter's Academy Vol. 2*, Class 230 (page 24) for a review. Even though the units are made with straight strips, they are sewn together at an angle and become on point once trimmed. Now, instead of a straight measurement that can easily be divided into the side measurement needed, you will be dealing with the square measurement multiplied by 1.414. Fractions can get messy with this process, making it a bit harder to make things fit exactly. You will find in many old quilts that the end of the border is just cut off wherever it ended instead of turning the corner accurately. This is one way to alleviate the frustration of mathematically figuring out sizes, but it is not always the best look. What is charming in old quilts seems to be judged harshly when repeated in our new quilts.

We placed a chart at the beginning of the chapter that will help you understand the strange decimal numbers you will be getting and allow you to figure out when to round up or down, and how much.

Let's start with simple squares on point. This is a real favorite with most quiltmakers, and we see it in use from the oldest quilts we have (eighteenth century) to today. It is fairly simple to plan and construct, and easy to change the size.

To start with the measuring, remember that the diagonal of a square is the straight side of the square multiplied by 1.414, which equals the measurement corner to corner diagonally.

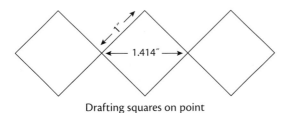

Drafting squares on point

1″ = 1.414″ diagonally

1½″ = 2.121″ diagonally

2″ = 2.828″ diagonally

You can see where the math can get a bit messy. When you have a given length that the border needs to be to fit the edge of the quilt top, the sizes generally don't come out as even numbers. There are a couple of different ways to work with this problem.

Start by measuring the width and length of the quilt top across the center, not along the edges. Subtract ½″ from each measurement for seam allowances. This gives you the finished width and length needed.

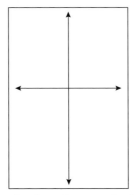

Measuring through center of quilt top

note We are assuming here that the corners will be added as an extra block, so we don't have to take into account measuring for the added length of the corners to the top and bottom borders.

If you have an idea of what size grid would look best in this border for your quilt, you can start with that measurement. As an example, say you have a quilt top that now needs four borders 36″ long. You think a 1½″ grid will look best for this border.

$$1.5″ \times 1.414 = 2.121″$$

$$36″ \div 2.121″ = 16.97″$$

This is a good number, as 0.97 is so close to the next full number that it will be easy to fit 17 squares onto the sides of the quilt accurately. Whenever you can round up or round down just a slight amount, it is doable.

What if your measurements don't turn out so well? Let's work with quilt top measurements of 24″ × 30″.

$1.5″ \times 1.414 = 2.121″$ divided into 24 = 11.31″ repeats—yikes! How do you deal with 0.31″?

$1.5″ \times 1.414 = 2.121″$ divided into 30 = 14.14″ repeats. Better, but not fun.

So, here are your options. Take the time to work with the calculator and see what grid might give you an even number of repeats you can work with, or think about adding a spacer border to change the numbers to ones that will work out evenly.

If you stay with the above numbers, it is known that you need to add a bit to each side to get an even repeat pattern. If you could have 12 repeats and 15 repeats, life would be happier. That means you need to add a spacer border to elongate each side, but how wide should they be?

$$12 \times 2.121″ = 25.45″ \text{ or almost } 25½″.$$

$$15 \times 2.121″ = 31.81″ \text{ or almost } 32″.$$

Using this method, you find that a ¾″ strip added to the 24″ side, and a 1″ strip added to the 30″ side will give you the measurements you need.

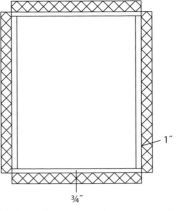

¾″

Adding strips to extend measurements

Chain of Squares on Point

We will start with the strip method, but realize that all the squares and backgrounds will be the same colors. This is not a technique to use if you want a scrappy look.

Once you know what the grid of the square is, use that measurement and add ½″ for the cut width of the strip that creates the squares. Add ¼″ to ½″ to this measurement for the width to cut the background strips.

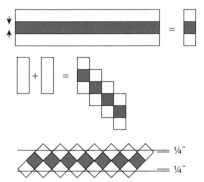

Strip sequence for squares on point border

Sew two strips together, iron toward the color, and starch. Measure the width of each strip and trim if necessary. Add the third strip and repeat the ironing and starching. Measure and trim again.

Cut the strip set into segments. The length is equal to the cut width of the strips. Make sure that you are measuring off the seams, not the outside edges. These cuts *must* be extremely accurate. Join pairs, right sides together, offsetting the segments by one square and matching the seams. We would suggest that you fan and iron each pair as you go. Sew the pairs into fours, then fours into eights, and so on, fanning and ironing with each addition. Remember that the edges

are bias, so be very gentle with the pieces so the edges don't become stretched or out of square.

Trim the long edges, measuring very carefully off each corner of the squares ¼″ for a seam allowance.

Scrappy Chain of Squares

There are two approaches to scrappy squares on point. The math is the same for figuring the sizes needed as above. The traditional method is to attach triangles to opposite sides of the squares, then join the units together. The main drawback to this method is working with small triangles, and keeping the long side of the triangle true. This edge tends to dip in a bit, not leaving enough width for the seam allowance. We suggest that you cut the triangles a bit too large so they can be trimmed. This method allows you to use a lot of different fabrics for the triangles.

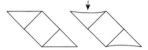

The second method is similar to strip piecing in that you can avoid sewing individual triangles onto the sides of squares, but you will need to sew a strip and then rectangles onto the square instead. There are a couple of extra steps involved, but you avoid having to cut and deal with triangles. With both methods you have the option of using as many different squares as you want.

You will still cut background strips, but instead of sewing three strips together, you will be adding squares to the strip, leaving a small space between each square. Be sure to leave enough room to enable you to square the segments. Cut these units apart and iron toward the square.

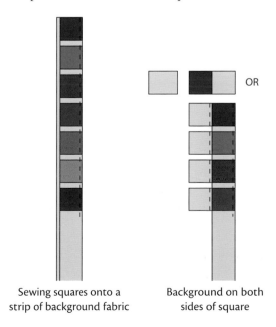

Sewing squares onto a strip of background fabric

Background on both sides of square

Cut the background unit to be exactly as wide as the square.

Next, cut rectangles for the opposite side of the square. They will be as long as the background strip was cut wide, and as wide as the square. Attach these to the opposite side of the square. Iron toward the square.

If you prefer to use a strip, sew the opposite side of the square onto another strip of background fabric, leaving the same small space as before. Cut the units apart and iron toward the square once again. Square this side as you did the first.

Carefully cut the background even with the square. The unit needs to be straight, square, and exact. Once it is trimmed, offset a unit with the first unit as you did in the strip technique. Match the seams and sew them together. Continue with pairs, then fours, and so on, until the border strip is the correct length. Carefully do the final ironing, and then trim the background away to ¼" from the points of the squares.

Trimming strips

note Even though most books tell their readers to avoid bias at all costs, here are times that bias is a real helper for fitting a border onto given measurements. Bias is pliable, and while it does stretch easily, this is an advantage when you need a small fraction extra at the ends to make the border fit. That tiny bit of give works to your advantage. On the other hand, if you need to shorten it a tiny bit, using a bit of starch and the heat of the iron will shrink up the edge just a bit and you will never know you were a bit long. When you do this, spray the starch onto the edge, and slowly lower the iron (no steam) onto the border. If you have the border pinned onto the edge of the quilt top, you can see how much you need to pull in. Do this in several places to ease it in naturally. Another way to deal with very slight fullness is to sew with the pieced border on the bottom so it has contact with the feed dogs. Pin every 2" or so, then let the feed dogs ease in the fullness. The more you work with these crazy decimal point measurements, the more you will learn how to fudge to make everything work out perfectly.

This is the joy of making medallion quilts. It is an adventure to figure out the puzzle. Now you get to pick the fabric that will set this border apart from the previous one and add another element of design to the quilt. What fun!!

As you design your own medallion quilts, this is the process. Drawing each round of borders out on graph paper is almost mandatory so that you can get an idea of how each border will fit and where you will need to add the plain strips to extend the size when necessary.

When working with this border, you can either use a square on point in each corner to continue the design, or use a quarter-triangle unit at each end and use a half-square triangle for the corner square. This lends a bit of variety to the border and is a striking variation.

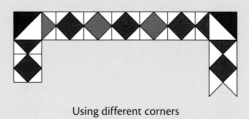

Using different corners

note If you are familiar with Seminole piecing, you will see that we are utilizing its techniques in these borders. Much of the terminology is the same but there is a slight difference as construction develops. Strip sets and segments are the same as we are used to, but as the segments are combined, they are called sections. Once all the sections are sewn together, the finished unit is called a band instead of a border. Harriet did a lot of Seminole piecing in the 1980s and learned quite a few tricks for making more complex borders in an easier manner. The only thing to be careful of is cutting angles. If the cutting gets off, the entire pattern will be affected. You will see this technique through this entire section. If you are interested in learning more about Seminole piecing, two of our favorite books are The Seminole Patchwork Book by Cheryl Greider Bradkin and Simply Seminole by Dorothy Hanisko.

MOSAIC BORDERS

Mosaic borders are simply more repeats of more rows of squares on point

The color changes this border lets you do can add a lot of excitement to the design. The following border designs are different because of the number of colors used and their placement. There are several ways to color the mosaic border. The math to figure out grid size is the same as for squares on point, but you just have to measure both direction this time, as the more rows you add the wider the border gets by the diagonal measurement. The wider the border gets, the smaller the grid needs to be. These borders are wonderful in a 1″ grid. Double and triple are standard, but you can add as many as you need and want. Draw out a line drawing and color in your own colors.

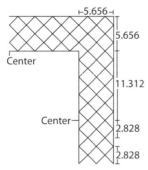

Line drawing of 2″ grid, three-row mosaic border

This illustration shows the corner treatment as well as the diagonal measurements of the pieces along the edge. You can see where the math gives you irregular measurements along the edge. If you add up the totals from the corner to either center mark (this is a square quilt), you will get 16.968, or 17″. If you mistakenly added the grid measurement instead of the diagonal measurement, you would only get 12″.

When attaching the border to the edge of the quilt top, the center of one side triangle would be placed at the center of the length of the edge the border is being added to. This side measurement is 1.414 of the size of the square.

Let's review the math again. First, measure the edge the border will need to fit. Next, determine how large you want the squares to be in the border.

Example: You want 1½″ squares within the border. The diagonal measurement of a 1½″ square is

$$1.5″ \times 1.414 = 2.121″$$

The quilt top is 45″ square. Divide 45″ by 2.121″ = 21.216. This lets you know that you would need 21 squares on point to fill the space, but you will have 0.216 of a square of extra space. You can probably ease this amount throughout the length of the border, especially since the edges are bias.

Another option is to change the grid size of the square:

1¼″ = 1.25″ × 1.414 = 1.767″

45″ divided by 1.767″ = 25.466— even more to deal with

1¾″ = 1.75″ × 1.414 = 2.474″

45″ divided by 2.474″ = 18.189— a minute amount to deal with

2″ = 2″ × 1.414 = 2.828″

45″ divided by 2.828″ = 15.912

As you look at the possibilities, the 1½″ and the 1¾″ sizes look easiest to work with. Now you will need to make the decision as to which one will look best with your fabric choices and quilt design. As all this comes together, you will need to also consider the width the border is going to be. The larger the squares, the wider the border. If you use a 1½″ grid, the two rows would total 4¼″ wide. The 1¾″ grid finishes to almost 5″. Is this going to be too wide for your design? Sometimes the borders can become overwhelming to the quilt just because of the grid size. How about a 1″ or 1⅛″ grid? Play with your calculator and see if you can start to get a feel for the scale change with each grid size change. Again, graph paper is your best friend when designing medallion quilts.

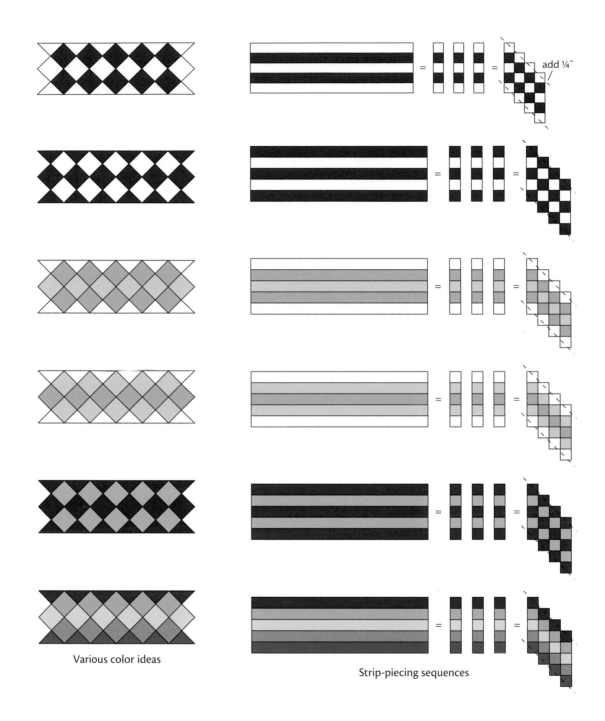

add ¼"

Various color ideas

Strip-piecing sequences

note To determine the width of the strips, use the grid measurement plus ½" for seam allowances, not the diagonal measurement. Always add ¼" to ½" to the outside (or background) strip for seam allowance. Cut the segments the same width as the strip width for the squares.

A Few More Ideas

You get to the point where you don't know where to stop when coloring in border ideas. Here are a few more to add to your collection.

Instead of an odd number of units in the border, how about using an even number? Below is an example.

This border is scrappy. It requires using short strip sets and fewer repeats of the same color combinations. It could also have more random color placement, making it even scrappier.

Changing the color of the outside units to blend with the fabrics they are sewn next to can give a floating effect to the row of squares. The color of the outside units can be used to frame or blend, whichever you need it to do in its position in the quilt.

Instead of plain blocks, use four-patch blocks in the border.

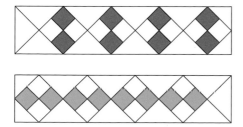

The position of the color can impact the effect of the design.

Once the four-patches are constructed, join them together using spacers. Cut strips of the background fabric the width of the unfinished four-patch units. Cut these strips into segments twice as long as the four-patch units. Sew the four-patches to the ends of the segments. Cut at a 45° angle equidistant between the seamlines. Attach the end piece of the last segment back to the beginning of the strip.

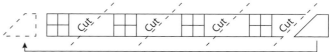

Turn the sections on end and stitch edge to edge, matching seamlines. Square the ends. This is a great way to add variety to the edges of the border. Because it is constructed with segments instead of strips, the segments can be scrappy, giving you a chance to use a large variety of fabrics.

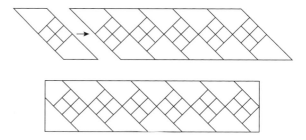

Try using nine-patch blocks instead of four-patch units.

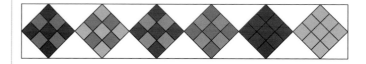

Any pieced block can be used with this method, which is so much easier than cutting triangles and trying to get them even at the edges.

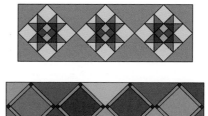

The traditional method for joining these units is to add individual triangles to opposite sides of the blocks, then sew them together. If you choose this method, the measurement for the triangle is the size of the block unfinished multiplied by 1.414. That measurement is the size of square needed, cut in half diagonally, for the side triangles. We have found that to cut them larger than needed helps us keep them exactly straight when trimming. When cut to size, there is no fudge room. We also never do this process without using Marti Michell's Perfect Patchwork Corner Trimmer. By having the special angle cut at the points, they always line up correctly.

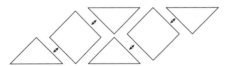

Adding triangles instead of strip sewing

Let's go one step further and piece the triangles to add more interest.

Small and large squares used in border

What if we used Drunkard's Path units in the border? You could really get into some fun color combinations with this idea.

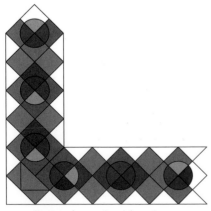

Curves thrown into the mixture

DIAGONAL STRIPS

Diagonal strips can add a lot of interest to a border. This is especially good for using up scrap strips. Below are a few we like.

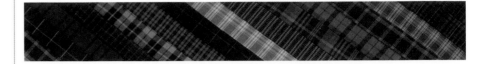

This border is made of strips cut as long as you want your border to be wide with extra added to the cut width of the strip for offsetting. If your border needs to be 4″ wide, and you want each strip to be 1″ wide, cut the strips 5¼″ long and 1½″ wide. When sewing the strips together, offset the ends by ¾″. Be sure to make a mark at this measurement so that each strip is in the correct position. Once all the strips are joined and ironed, cut the edges from inside point to inside point.

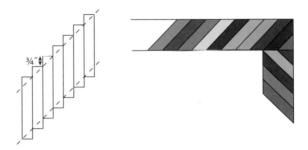

The following borders are striking in quilts. Singles, doubles, offset, and added bands between the piecing all make for a variety of designs to add to your quilt.

The next borders are constructed as strip sets, but with all but the first one, you will need to construct two mirror-image strip units. Changing size for this border is easy, as the finished width of the border is always twice the finished width of the strips. Let's break down the math again.

> *tip* This border can also be constructed with half-square triangles. The only problem with triangles is the seam that would then go through the diagonal shape. This would be a design choice as to which technique to use based on the fabric choice and how well it might camouflage the seams.

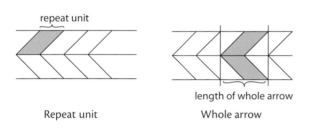

Repeat unit   Whole arrow

The repeat unit along the side of the border is 1.414 times the finished width of the strip. The length of the total arrow is the repeat unit plus the finished width of one strip.

2″ finished border = 1½″ cut width of strip = 1″ finished width of strip × 1.414 = 1.41″ repeat + 1″ (finished strip) = 2.41″ length of complete arrow

3″ finished border = 2″ cut width of strip = 1.5″ finished width of strip × 1.414 = 2.12″ repeat + 1.5″ (finished strip) = 3.62″ length of complete arrow

4″ border width = 2½″ cut width of strip = 2″ finished width of strip × 1.414 = 2.83 + 2″ (finished strip) = 4.82″ length of complete arrow

When constructing the strip sets, be sure to turn one around and cut from the opposite angle to create a mirror image when the segments are sewn together.

> *tip* To save a bit of fabric, stair-step each strip unit. Measure in the distance of the finished width of the strip and start the next strip at this mark. For example, if your strips are cut 2″, step the next strip in 1½″ from the end.

> *tip* Iron the seam allowances one direction on one strip set, but the opposite direction on the second strip set that will be cut mirrored to the first.

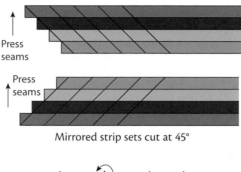

Press seams

Press seams

Mirrored strip sets cut at 45°

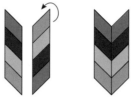

Cut segments turned to create arrows

Once all the segments are cut from the strip sets, sew into pairs and continue until you arrive at the length needed. You will be sewing the ends of the segments together at an angle, so review this process in *Volume 1*, Piecing Borders (page 97), if you have trouble keeping the strips straight.

Once you determine how wide your border will be and how many arrows are needed for the length, square the end of each long strip by adding background triangles. Cut a square the size of the cut segment and cut in half diagonally.

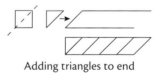

Adding triangles to end

These ends can be used as the center to change direction of the arrows or as a blunt end when a different block is used for the corner squares.

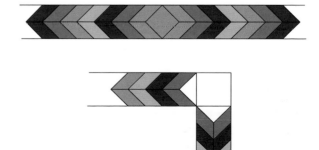

For an unbroken corner, add a corner triangle to a mitered corner of the two borders.

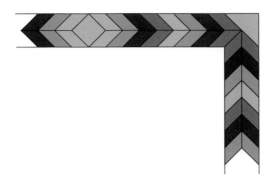

STACKED BRICKS

Another border that is simple shapes cut at an angle is the Stacked Bricks border. This border is another strip border, with the appearance of bricks leaning against one another.

Stacked Bricks

If you want all the bricks to be the same color, strip piecing is the easiest way to go.

Determine what width will look best on your quilt top. The bricks can be rectangles of almost any size you want. Once you determine the finished size of the bricks, add ½″ to the *length* of the brick for seam allowance. Cut the brick fabric strip this wide (center strip). Add ½″ to the width of the finished rectangle to find the segment cut width. Cut the background strips ½″ wider than the *segment* cut width.

Example:

You have decided that small bricks look best for your project—2″ × 4″ finished. Cut the brick strip 4½″ wide and the background strips 3″ wide. The segment cuts would be 2½″ wide.

For smaller bricks—1½″ × 3″—the brick strip would be cut 3½″ wide and the background strips would be cut 2½″ wide. The segments are cut 2″ wide.

If you want a 3″ × 5″ brick border, the brick strip would be 5½″ wide and the background strips 4″ wide. The segment cuts would be 3½″ wide.

With this formula, you can make the bricks any size that you need to fit the edge of your quilt top. On graph paper, try making the bricks narrower than above, but the same length. You will see how the proportions are affected by the measurements. Experiment until you find one that is pleasing on your quilt top.

One thing to consider when choosing your brick size is how wide the border will be with that brick size. Let's go back to 1.414. To get the width measurement, look at the illustrations and you will see that there are 1½ squares making up the width. You will need to take the 1.414 answer and multiply it by 1½ to get the width.

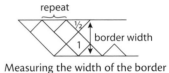

Measuring the width of the border

Below is a list of border widths at different brick sizes:

1½″ bricks = 1.5″ × 1.414 = 2.121″ × 1.5 = 3.181″

2″ bricks = 2″ × 1.414 = 2.828″ × 1.5 = 4.242″

2½″ bricks = 2.5″ × 1.414 = 3.535″ × 1.5 = 5.30″

3″ bricks = 3″ × 1.414 = 4.242″ × 1.5 = 6.363″

The size of the bricks is one part of the equation, but so is the width of the border. Don't forget that the bricks can be made long and skinny instead of in a 1:2 ratio (1½″ × 3″), as we have used in the examples. If you want narrow, skinny bricks, say in a 1:3 ratio (1½″ × 4½″), the border could be wider with more narrow bricks. This might appear less bulky for your quilt than wide bricks. Play with different ratios on graph paper and see what pleases your style.

Another consideration as you are deciding on what size to make your bricks is to look at the borders and how the corners are formed when added to the quilt top. The length of the border needed might affect the size of the bricks you decide on.

Each border strip will begin and end with one segment. They are not squared off at the ends as we have been doing on other borders, but instead are either mitered or capped off with more bricks. We will discuss this after the piecing process is covered.

The finished length of each side of the quilt top must be equal to the number of finished segment repeats. Using the sizes of 1½" × 3" bricks, you would start by determining the side measurement of the background triangles. If the segments were cut 2", the finished measurement would be 1½". The diagonal of 1½" (the triangles on the edge) is 1.5" × 1.414 = 2.121".

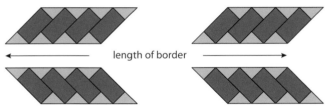
length of border

Measuring for border length

The length of each side of the quilt top must equal the number of attached segments in the border. An example would be to have 15 segments sewn together with 1½" bricks. With the diagonal measurement at 2.121" and 15 segments, the length of the border would be 31.8". If you need a border to be 36" long, adding another 2 segments would fit. 17 × 2.121" = 36.057". We like to have the completed border length to within ⅛" to ¼" larger or smaller. We know we can work with that to make it fit. By adding the extra 2 segments, we are spot on.

By continually working the numbers, you will be able to get the length border you need, with the size bricks you want, and know how many segments you need to make.

Construction

To construct the bricks, start by sewing the strips together. Iron the seams toward the center strip. Draw a line on the wrong side of the brick strip down the center. This line will be used for placement of the segments when joining them together.

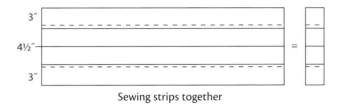
3"
4½"
3"

Sewing strips together

Cut the segments perpendicular to the seams, keeping the ruler aligned with the seams.

Join the segments by placing the top seam of one segment on the centerline of the brick strip of the first segment. This centers the stagger of the bricks. You will need to stagger the sides of the quilt down, and the top and bottom borders up.

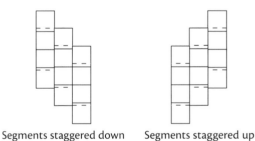

Segments staggered down   Segments staggered up

Once the segments are joined, iron the seam allowances in one direction, being very careful not to distort and stretch the edges. Trim the long edges ¼" from the points of the bricks.

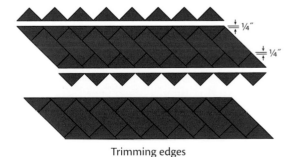
¼"
¼"

Trimming edges

If you want a scrappy look, use many different fabrics in shorter strip units, then attach them randomly to each other. You can also alternate two colors, or a sequence of colors.

There are two different ways to handle the corners for the Stacked Bricks border. One method will give you two different corners on the quilt. This method keeps all the bricks lying at the same angle on all sides of the quilt top. In this example, the bricks are staggered down in the side borders and up in the top and bottom borders.

Capped

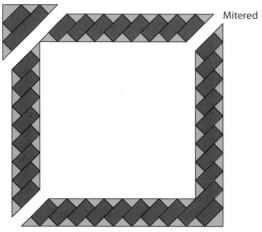
Mitered

Two different corners

When the borders are attached to the quilt top, the two corners with miters need to have the borders stitched to the ¼" seamline so that you can create and sew the miter. The opposite corners are capped off with finishing triangle units. To make these units, cut 2 bricks that are twice the length of the bricks in the border and the same width (unfinished) as the border bricks, plus ½". Cut 2 squares the width of the bricks and attach to the ends of the long bricks. Iron toward the bricks. Make 2 additional brick units the same size as the border bricks. The measurement of the smaller brick plus ½" is the diagonal measurement of the triangle needed for the corner. Divide this measurement by 1.414 to find the size square needed. Cut in half diagonally for the corners.

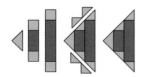
Steps to creating two corners

Be sure to carefully center the smaller brick on the longer brick. Add the corner triangle and trim to ¼" from the brick points.

The opposite corners are mitered. Carefully align the seams, reironing if butting the seams helps you keep them at a true 45° angle.

An optional way to handle the corners is to make them the same, using the capping method above, but reversing the direction of the bricks in the center of each border. This would make each border use half staggered up and half staggered down units.

Cut 4 squares the size of the segment cut. Multiply that measurement by 1.414 to get the size square you need for the background. Cut 4 of these squares. Cut them in half diagonally. Construct the unit in the illustration below.

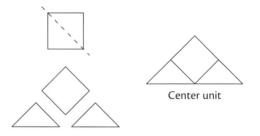
Center unit

Remove one background triangle from one of the border halves as illustrated below. Sew the new unit onto the end of this border half, and then add the other half on the other side of the center unit.

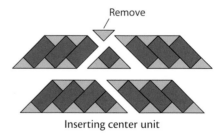
Remove

Inserting center unit

Sew the four borders onto the edges of the quilt top. Cap each corner with the new units.

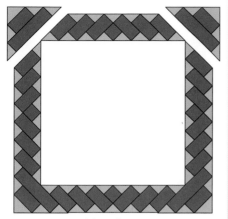

Position of corners

If you want to have fun with a lot of scraps and a totally different look for stacked brinks, consider piecing three-piece triangle units. If you are careful with the color and value placement of the fabrics, you get the appearance of bricks but not the repetitive use of one color. With careful planning of color, this is a striking border.

Three-piece triangles used to make Stacked Bricks

SAWTOOTH BORDERS

This is a favorite border of most quilters and found on endless quilts. It is straightforward and easy to fit onto most dimensions of the quilt top. The repeat is small and there are a myriad of ways to set the half-square triangles to make many different designs.

We covered eight different methods for making half-square triangles in *Quilter's Academy Vol. 3,* so please refer back to that book for instructions for making perfect half-square triangles of any size you need.

Below is a gallery of designs using just half-square triangles. Some of the designs will be revisited for other techniques later in the chapter. As you are designing your quilt, take into consideration where the seam allowances are, how much they show, and if they will cause confusion with the way you want to quilt the border. When two half-square triangles are placed side by side with the same color touching, the seam breaks the image of a large triangle in this area. If this is a design problem, read on and you will find alternative ways of getting the same shapes with different units.

Single Sawtooth Borders

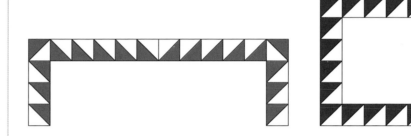

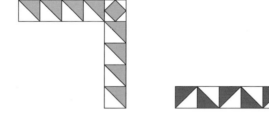

Double Sawtooth Borders

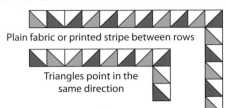

Plain fabric or printed stripe between rows

Triangles point in the
same direction

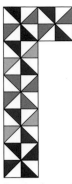

Alternating triangles for a pinwheel effect

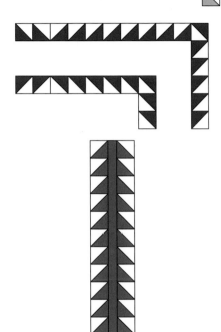

Different spacing between sawtooth borders

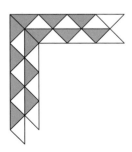

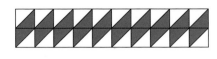

note Any time two half-square triangle units are placed together to make a parallelogram, the easiest method is to cut a rectangle and sew and flip squares on the ends to create the angle. If you are not familiar with this technique, refer to Quilter's Academy Vol. 3, Class 310, Lesson Four (pages 14–16).

The use of three rows of sawtooth borders around a center can be striking. The size of the triangles can be a factor affecting the success of this border, as too small may appear busy and too large overpowering.

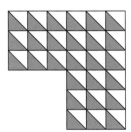

You can mix things up a bit by using a pieced triangle unit joined to a large triangle for a broken sawtooth border.

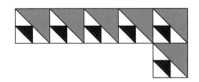

DOGTOOTH BORDERS

Below are a variety of dogtooth borders. These pieces can be combined with half-square triangles and squares in the corners, and can point in different directions.

Single Dogtooth Borders

Single dogtooth border

Zigzag dogtooth border

Dogtooth borders can be made by sewing half-square triangles together, but as suggested earlier and shown in the illustration above, the joining seams in the centers, where the same colors come together, is distracting.

Triangle Template Method

We prefer this method for borders that are wider than 2″. When larger triangles are rotary or template cut, it is fast and straightforward. The larger triangles fill space quickly. It is also very easy to put together a scrappy-looking border using individual triangles.

This is the most common way to make this border—individual triangles sewn end to end. Without the help of the Corner Trimmer (from Perfect Patchwork Templates), it is very time consuming and hard to get the outside edges to come out straight and have a ¼″ seam allowance beyond all the points along the edge. We strongly suggest that you take the time to cut the corners with the template to make this border fast and accurate.

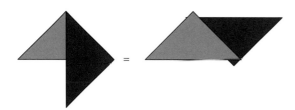

Points are too close together

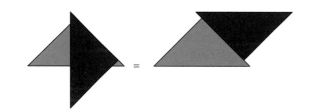

Points are too far apart

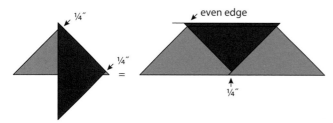

Points correctly positioned

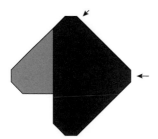

Template angles that align points
and corners for perfect fit

Strip-Piecing Method

This border can be a very small accent to a wider, stronger statement. We prefer to appliqué the points when they get to 1″ or smaller to eliminate having a seam beyond the points. This will depend on where you place this border. Seminole piecing makes creating the more narrow borders easy and efficient. When wider borders are needed, we suggest that you go back to the template method. It is fast and the large triangles fill space quickly.

This is a strip technique. Below is a chart of strip sizes for different widths of borders. If you need exact widths, go back to the triangle template method above. These measurements are odd in order to keep the strip width in easy ruler numbers. To determine the size needed, remember that the long side of the triangle is giving the border the length. After deciding on a corner treatment, measure the quilt top edge and figure how many triangles are needed to fill that measurement.

Changing Size of Dogtooth Border Using Seminole Technique

Border width	Unit repeat	Dogtooth strip	Background strip	Segment cut width
0.88″	1.76″	2″	2″	1¾″
1.06″	2.12″	2¼″	2¼″	2″
1.24″	2.47″	2½″	2½″	2¼″
1.41″	2.83″	2¾″	2¾″	2½″
1.59″	3.18″	3″	3″	2¾″
1.77″	3.54″	3¼″	3¼″	3″

Once you choose the size you want to make, cut a strip each from two fabrics the width designated on the chart. We will be working with the 2½″ strip size, giving us a 1¼″-wide border.

Sew the 2 strips together and iron seam toward the side. On the side you have ironed toward, draw a line ½″ from the top edge of the strip. Cut the strip set into 2¼″ segments.

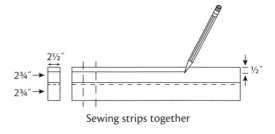

Sewing strips together

Join the segments into pairs, matching the line you drew on one unit to the seam of the next unit.

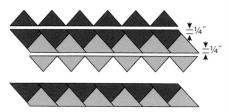

Joining segments

Sew the pairs into fours, and so on, until you have enough for one edge of your quilt top. Iron all seam allowances in the same direction. Trim the edges, leaving a ¼″ seam allowance beyond points.

Trimming edges

Dogtooth borders have a ton of design potential, and once you see that they are fairly easy to make, they might become one of your favorite border designs.

When the dogtooth border is made up of two rows, it looks completely different. The first illustration shows how a zigzag is created when they are all the same color. This is often called Streak of Lightning.

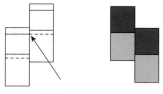

Zigzag border

When two fabrics are used in the same way, a very different look is obtained.

Using two colors

Below are three illustrations of double dogtooth borders with a space between two single dogtooth borders. The distance between the two borders can be any distance you want or need, or a wonderful print or printed strip could be showcased between the two sets of points, especially the two where the points are pointing in or out. Notice the different corner treatments and how they change the impact on the border.

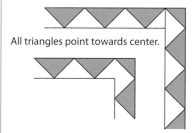

All triangles point towards center.

All triangles point toward center of quilt

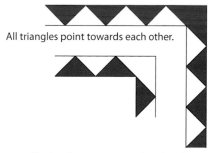

All triangles point towards each other.

All triangles point toward each other

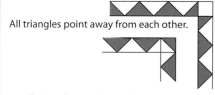

All triangles point away from each other.

All triangles point away from each other

The two borders below really add a lot of punch to the dogtooth design. Adding a matching straight border to the inside of the dogtooth border, then appliquéd circles in that space, increases the border interest dramatically.

Color placement and adding circles

If one of the dogtooth elements is internally pieced as shown below, you get a totally new idea.

Internal piecing of one triangle unit

Quarter-Square Triangle Borders

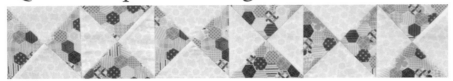

This is a straightforward use of quarter-square units. They can be all the same color or scrappy, and positioned in a straight line or with every other unit turned half a turn. This is an easy border to make in any size from large to small. We covered making quarter-square triangles in *Quilter's Academy Vol. 3*, Lesson Two (page 55) if you need a review.

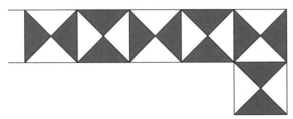

Alternating quarter-square triangles

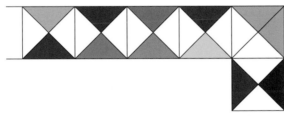

Using different fabrics to create a scrappy look

Flying Geese Borders

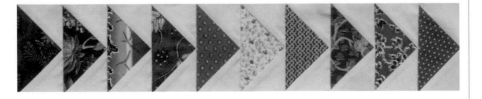

Flying Geese borders are probably one of the most used and recognized borders in older medallion quilts. These units can be positioned to make a myriad of different patterns.

SINGLE FLYING GEESE BORDERS

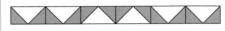

IDEAS FOR CORNER TREATMENT

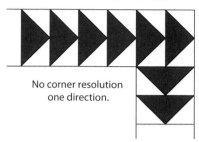

No corner resolution one direction.

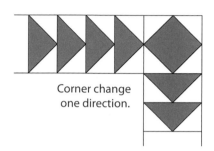

Corner change one direction.

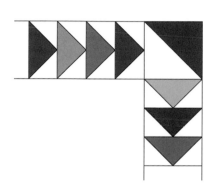

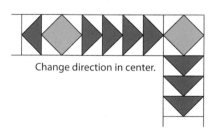

Change direction in center.

Quilter's Academy Vol. 3 instructs you in four different methods to make Flying Geese units, so we have decided to not repeat that information here. Refer back to *Volume 3*, Class 350 (pages 69–75) for detailed instructions.

Zigzag Borders

Like sawtooth and dogtooth borders, the zigzag borders have many variations. We are going to give three different zigzag border techniques: Ribbons, Peaks, and Streak of Lightning. The strip that makes the center diagonal line is what is referred to as the *ribbon*, the *peak*, or the *streak of lightning*. We are going to refer to this strip as a *ribbon* in the rest of this unit to keep it simple. Depending on the width of the border, the size of the ribbon, color changes, and number of ribbons, you can play with this border for a long time and come up with exactly what you need for your quilt.

Outline of zigzag shape

Once the angles are established for the zigzag, design elements, colors, and construction techniques can be changed.

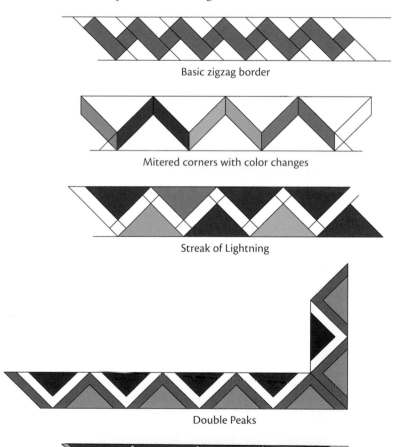

Basic zigzag border

Mitered corners with color changes

Streak of Lightning

Double Peaks

Skinny Streak

There are three different approaches to this border, some using the Seminole piecing idea of using strips and others using strips and triangles. As you look at various elements of the above pieced borders, you can imagine that before machine piecing and all our speed techniques, this border could have been tedious and time consuming. With strip methods, life is much better.

> *tip* These borders can be difficult to work out to the right length to enable turning balanced corners. This might be a good time to consider using corner squares as a design element instead of continuous corners.

Twisted Ribbon Borders

Two-color Twisted Ribbon

Double Twisted Ribbons with appliquéd circles

This is a quick method when you want a zigzag border, and if you want to give a twisted look to the ribbon by using two different fabrics and the same background. This is a common border seen in contemporary quilts, so we are starting here to learn how to measure and draft the borders to determine size and fit.

This border has to be measured along the side to find the repeat. Because the edge is the diagonal of a triangle,

the 1.414 equations are used again. Below is a diagram of where the pattern repeat is.

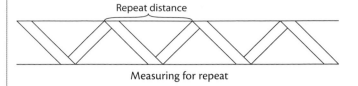

Measuring for repeat

The border *width* is half the size of the repeat. If the repeat is 4¼″ long, the border width will be 2.12″ wide. You can see where planning the width of the strips can be confusing with this border because of the addition of the ribbon. We strongly suggest again that you draft out the size you want your border to be and get exact measurements. You can also work it out on graph paper.

Let's try to figure out how to get a 4″ border (diagrammed below). We want the ribbon to be 1″ wide. Looking at the diagram, we see that along the edge, the ribbon is cut at a 45° angle, so its measurement is $1″ \times 1.414 = 1.414″$. We want a 4″ border. If the diagonal measurement were 1.414″, half of that would be the height of the small triangle formed where the two ribbons come together, 0.70″, or ¾″. Subtract ¾″ from 4″ and we get 3¼″. This would be half the length of the diagonal measurement of the triangle between the ribbons. Therefore, if the ribbon is 1.414″ and the triangle is 6½″, the repeat would be 7.91″. If our formula is right—the repeat is twice as long as the width—this would be very close. As you know, we never come up with perfect, even numbers when working with diagonals. This is close enough.

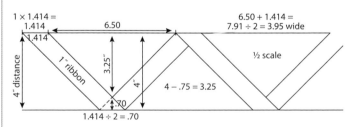

Graph paper showing where measurements are derived

Let's do one more. We want the border to be about 3″ wide with a ¾″ ribbon.

$0.75″ \times 1.414 = 1.06$, or 1″

$1″ \div 2 = 0.5″$ or ½″

$3″ - 0.5 = 2.5″$ or 2½″

$2.5″ \times 2 - 5″$ (the length of the triangle)

$5″ + 0.75″ = 5.75″ \div 2 = 2.87″$, very close to 3″

The repeat measurement would be 8″. If you want your ribbon to be 1″ wide, subtract 1.414″ from 8 = about 6½″. That is the long side of the triangle. Half that distance is the height of the triangle—3¼″—plus the 1.414″ for the ribbon = 4.66″.

Now we need to figure out the measurements to cut the strips of fabric. We know that the ribbon is 1″ wide in our 4″ border, so the ribbon fabric(s) would be cut 1½″ wide. If you look at the drawing below, you will see that you have to extend the triangle units quite a ways beyond the edge of the strip to accommodate the angle of the finished edge. We have allowed plenty of extra seam allowance to get a straight cut when trimming. The measurements add up to 5½″-wide strips for the triangle fabric.

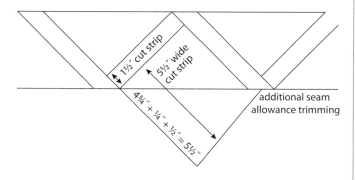

When constructing the strip set, iron seam allowances toward the ribbon. On the wrong side of the fabric, draw a line ½″ above the top seam and ½″ below the bottom seam on the background (triangle) fabric. Cut the segments 5⅛″ wide.

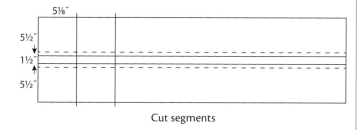

Cut segments

Cut additional strips of ribbon fabric 1½″ wide and subcut into 7¾″-long pieces.

Position the top edge of the strip with the top drawn line of one segment. Iron toward the strip. Align the bottom edge of the strip with the bottom line on another segment and attach. Iron toward the strip. If this strip is too short or too long, the stagger will be off, as will be the angle of the ribbons and the shape of the triangle.

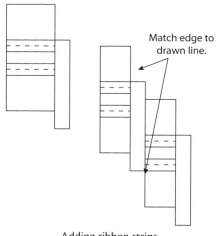

Match edge to drawn line.

Adding ribbon strips

> **tip** To double-check your math, make a test run and check the position of the ribbon across the segments. The finished width of the segment should be the same as the distance between the segment ribbons when staggered. This area needs to be square in order to create a true triangle when trimmed.

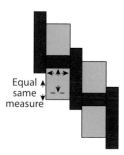

Equal same measure

When joining the segments, stagger the pieces down for two of the borders and up for the other two.

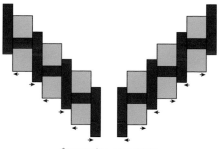

Staggering segments

Trim the long edges, leaving ¼″ seam allowances.

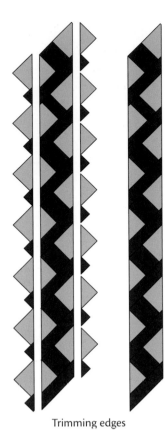

Trimming edges

CORNERS FOR RIBBON BORDERS

If you thought the math has been a bit difficult to get the border width, you might find that finding the exact length is a bit much. To get the corners of this border to turn perfectly, very careful planning and sizing must be done.

If you look at the illustration below, you will see that each border needs to end with the segment element of the border. When piecing your segments together, start and end with the segment, not the narrow strip. To check that you have the right size repeat to fit your quilt, divide the length of the quilt top edge by the repeat size of your drafted border. Check to make sure the segment element is at the ends of the measurement. If not, start again

and change the width of the ribbon or the width of the border to make the adjustment. Easier yet, consider adding a narrow strip to the quilt top to get that measurement to accommodate the border you want. You can work with up to a ⅛" to ¼" discrepancy.

> **note** *If you study antique quilts, and especially antique medallions, you will find that as often as not, the borders were not mathematically compatible to the edge they were sewn to. Quilters back then tended to just end the border wherever it needed to stop and cut it off. This can add quite a bit of interest to the quilt, but in today's world, this is not as acceptable as it was once. You do have the option of doing this anytime the math is just too much to bear. You will find that even with the most meticulous planning, things will not fit as exactly in fabric as drawn on graph paper. Just go with it and enjoy the process, and if all else fails, do as our foremothers did and just sew it on and keep going. This is also a good place to use a square corner to end the pattern.*

Once you have the borders sized to fit, sew them onto the four sides of the quilt top. Stop sewing ¼" from the edge of the two corners that will need to be mitered. These corners are simple miters that finish the corner turn.

For the two remaining corners, cut a strip of ribbon fabric the same width as the border. The length can be measured against the quilt top. Add a bit of extra length for squaring the ends. Sew this strip onto the corners. A triangle is added to the corner to square it off. The triangle size is the length of the strip you just added divided by 1.414. This gives you the size square to cut in half diagonally, giving you the triangles. Cut 2.

Center the triangles onto the corner and attach them to the strip. Trim the strip and triangle to be even with the outer edges of the border.

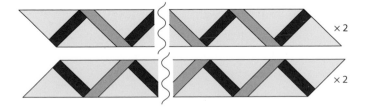

Turned corners

BASIC ZIGZAG

Strip-pieced zigzag border

This is a bold border based on Seminole piecing techniques. The turns are sharp and close together. The width of the zigzag could be changed to fit your needs with a bit of drafting and measuring. Use the formula in Twisted Ribbons to figure out the width and length of this border for your quilt project.

This is an easy and straightforward strip-pieced border. Unlike the Twisted Ribbon, the offset is a given and the stair step is small. Once you determine the size of border

you need, cut the strips to accommodate the background and the zigzag. There are two strip sets needed for this border design. For our example, we are using the dimensions for a 3″ (mathematically 2.82″) border with a 1″ zigzag.

Strip sets for 3″ border

Sew strip sets together, two strips at a time, ironing and starching as we always do. Trim each side to be exact and add third strip. Iron the seams of strip set A toward the background and strip set B toward the zigzag fabric.

Cut a 1½″ segment from all the strip sets.

Join the segments, alternating one by one, into pairs. Match the bottom seam. Continue sewing the pairs into fours, and so on. When the border is completed, carefully iron the seam allowances all one direction. Be very careful not to stretch the border as you iron, as everything is now bias.

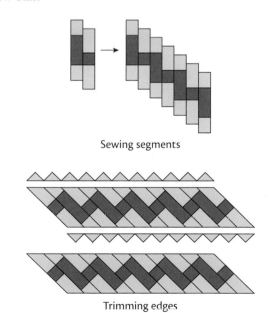

Sewing segments

Trimming edges

If you want to have the corners turn, each border strip must have a segment from strip set A at the left end and from strip set B at the right end. Remember that the repeat needs to be accounted for to make this border fit the corners correctly. Add triangles to the B ends to complete the edge of the border on the outside edge and trim to a 90° angle. All four corners are mitered.

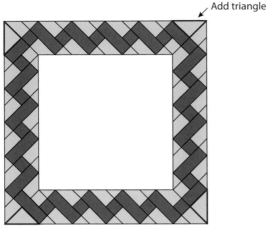

Add triangle

Border layout

PEAKS

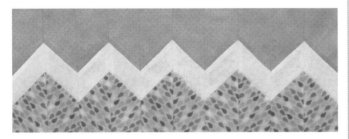

> *note* This is another simpler Seminole technique, but the drawback is the seam through the center of the large "triangle" position. If you are using a busy print fabric, this will probably not show. However, if a solid is used, the seam might interfere with the overall look of the finished border.

Start by determining how wide you want your border and how wide the ribbon will be, as well as how long you want each peak. This will determine the width of the segment cuts. The length of the peak will determine the width of the background strips. Draft out these sizes on graph paper so that you can determine the pattern repeat. Once you know the repeat measurement for your desired border, you can figure out how many segments are needed to make the border lengths you need. This will then tell you how many strip sets to construct.

Our example has a 1″-wide ribbon and the border is 6″ wide. This method is great when you want to extend the background beyond the ¼″ seam allowance. By making the background strips wider, you can have the edges any width you would like to make them. We cut the sample 3¼″ beyond each peak point on each side to give us a finished border 6″ wide. Cut strips of background fabric 2½″ wide and the ribbon fabric 1½″ wide. Segments are cut 2″ wide.

Sew equal numbers of strips together, stair-stepping in both directions (see illustration below).

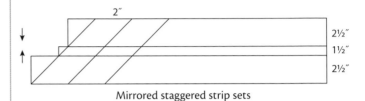

Mirrored staggered strip sets

Iron the seams of each strip set in opposite directions. This enables the seams to alternate when the segments are joined.

Cut the strips into 2″ segments, making sure that the 45° angle is exact with each cut.

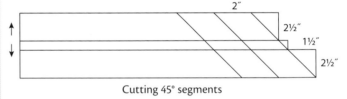

Cutting 45° segments

Stitch pairs of segments edge to edge, matching seamlines.

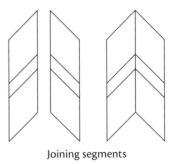

Joining segments

Once all the segments are joined, trim to your desired width from ribbon points, making sure the border remains exactly the same width the entire length of the piece.

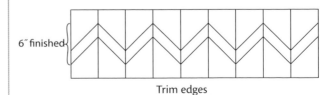

6″ finished

Trim edges

You can achieve a similar look using parallelograms. As illustrated above, these shapes have two sides that are longer than the other two. Because they are essentially two joined half-square triangles, the math is considerably easier than diamonds. If you want this look instead of true diamonds, you do not want to do Y-seaming, and you don't want all the seams you get when joining half-square triangles, you might want to consider making this border by sewing flipped corners onto rectangles. You will still get the seams in the center of the triangle, but this might make more sense to you. Word of caution though, you need to be extremely accurate with corners when sewing them or the corners won't turn accurately. If you want wider backgrounds, sew rectangles onto the rectangle instead of squares to extend the distance from the seam.

STREAK OF LIGHTNING BORDERS

This border looks very much like the ribbon borders, but this technique gives you the opportunity to use many different fabrics along the triangle edge, as each triangle can be cut and positioned individually, unlike the strip methods that repeat the same fabric.

Refer back to Twisted Ribbon Borders (page 120) and use the formula to figure out the size of the triangle and the strip that is needed to make your border size of choice. You will only need the first few steps for this technique.

Once you have determined the units' sizes, cut the triangles and the strips from as many different fabrics as you plan to use.

The issue of grainline needs to be addressed here. There are two ways of cutting the triangles for this quilt. One is to cut a square in half diagonally, which will result in a long bias edge on the edge of the border. Alternatively, you can cut a larger square into quarters, winding up with all the long triangle sides on the straight grain. Both methods can be defended.

If you need to ease or stretch the border minimally to make everything fit exactly, cutting on the bias would be helpful. As long as you are using starch every step of the way, the bias can be managed without a lot of trouble. Bias is easier to ease and work with when fitting than straight grain.

On the other hand, if you have trouble with your ironing and tend to stretch borders when working with them, bias would be like a rubber band! Stay with straight grain. This is totally your decision to make.

Grainline concerns

If you decide to cut straight-grain triangles, use the cut size of the short side of the triangle and multiply by 1.414, and you will have the size square needed for cutting into quarters.

Example:

For a 3¾"-wide border, the long side of the triangle is 6" finished. Add 1¼" for seam allowances to find the size of the square that is cut into quarters. If you want to find the size square to cut in half, use the 6" measurement divided by 1.414 (4.24"). That measurement plus a ⅞" seam allowance (4.24" + 0.875") would be a 5⅛" square, cut in half diagonally.

To construct this border, cut the ribbon strips the length of the short side of your triangle, squaring off the ends. Attach the strips to one short side of the triangles, making half of them the opposite way, mirroring the first half.

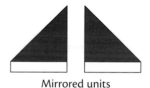

Mirrored units

Alternate the mirrored units and lay out the border. Sew pairs together first. Stitch from the lower edge of the triangle to about three-fourths of the way to the end. Leave this end open for the next step. Iron all seams toward the triangle.

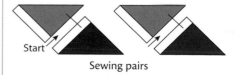

Start   **Sewing pairs**

 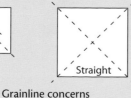

Align the blunt end of the unit you are adding to the end of the strip on the seam left open. Sew the units together.

Iron toward the triangle. Complete the unit by closing the seam that was left partially open. Iron.

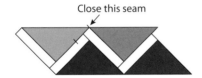

Close this seam

Diamond Borders

There are many variations of diamond borders. Some of the diamonds lie down and some stand up. Some can turn a corner and some can't. We are going to cover four basic diamond borders.

Lazy Diamonds

Diamonds at Attention

Half-Diamonds

Alternating Diamonds

A diamond is half as wide as it is long, so all the angles are 45°. If you were to cut a true diamond, you could fold it in half and it would line up exactly. Don't confuse true diamonds with parallelograms. These "diamonds" don't have equal sides. Two sides are longer than the other two. We will address these later. We are starting with one of the easiest but most stunning of the diamond borders.

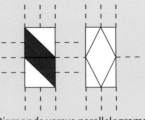

LAZY DIAMONDS

The design repeat for this border is the length of the diamond. We start out with the drafting to find the design repeat for the size border you want to create. This border can be any size, but the corners need to be considered when you are doing your planning. The corner treatment will affect the placement of the repeat in the border. Below are five different corner treatments.

 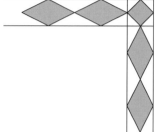

Anything can be put in the square.

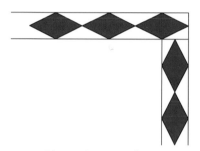 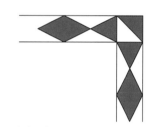

Diamonds run to edges.   Each border ends with a half-diamond.

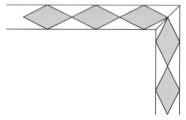

Diamond points meet at a mitered corner.

The first border example shows the diamond points ending at the edge of the quilt top, so the repeats need to fit into that space, adding a small plain border if necessary to get the width border you need.

The second border example has the side borders ending with points at the edge of the quilt, but the top and bottom borders go to the outside edge of the side borders. This might be quite a bit harder to make happen depending on the length of the diamonds.

Border example three ends the diamond repeat with a half-diamond, so the repeat is now the length of the background (also a diamond) instead of a full diamond.

Border four goes all the way into the corner, which is mitered.

Drafting these borders onto graph paper to work out the measurements is strongly suggested. Once drafted, you will see what needs to be adjusted or added to make the corners work.

To strip piece this border, figure what size strips you need. The background strip needs to be as wide as the diamond is long plus seam allowances. If we were making a 2″-wide border, the diamond would be 4″ long. If you draw this diamond on graph paper, you find that each side of the diamond measures 2¼″. Add ½″ and you have the width of the background strips, 2¾″ wide. The width of the diamond is 1¾″, needing a strip 2¼″ wide.

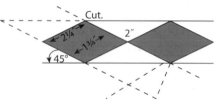

Draft your diamond size.

Sew the strips together. Offset the ends if you choose. Iron the seams toward the diamond fabric.

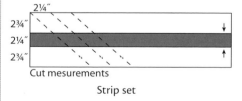

Cut mesurements

Strip set

We recommend that you use a 45° triangle ruler to cut segments. This helps you keep the angle exact by aligning the ruler lines on the two seams with each cut. Straight rulers tilt easily, and if the cuts are not exact, your diamonds won't be either. Carefully cut 2¼″ segments.

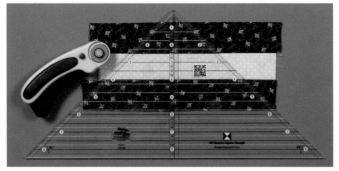
Cutting with triangle ruler

Join the segments into pairs, then fours, and so on, matching seams carefully.

Joining segments

> ### tip
> If you have problems matching these seams because of the 45°, use your Perkins Perfect Piecing Seam Guide to make a small mark on the seam allowance on the wrong side, showing you where you will be stitching from the edge. Use a pin to align both top and bottom unit right at the mark. Swing the pin around to take the stitch along one of the ironed seam allowances. This will help hold everything in place correctly. Clover Fine Patchwork Pins will let you sew over the pin so you don't have to remove it.

Iron all seams in the same direction. This is bias again, so work carefully. Trim the long edges, leaving a ¼″ seam allowance.

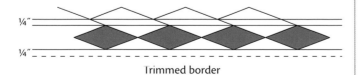
Trimmed border

> ### tip
> For some design fun, try drafting this border as a 60° diamond instead of a 45° diamond.

DIAMONDS AT ATTENTION

These diamonds are standing at attention on their points. This border can also be strip pieced. We are working with a 3″ border this time. The drafting below shows where we are getting our sizes for our strips and segments.

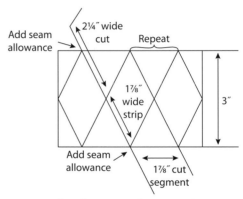
Drafting for Diamonds at Attention

Our measurements are 2¼″-wide background strips and 1⅞″-wide diamond strips. You might want to add a bit more to the background width for a little breathing room when trimming. Sew the strips together and iron toward the diamond strip. Check that each strip measures, finished, exactly what it should. Using the 45° ruler again, align it with the seams and cut 1⅞″ segments.

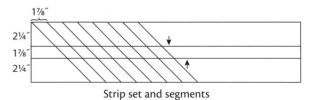
Strip set and segments

Stitch the segments together, matching the bottom seamline in one segment to the top seamline in the next. To square off the ends, add a wide strip of background to both ends and cut square.

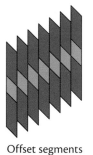 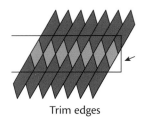

Offset segments   Trim edges

HALF-DIAMONDS (A.K.A. DOGTOOTH)

Another classic pattern is using half-diamonds.

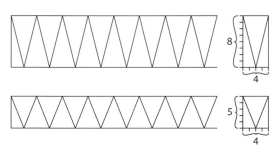

Half diamonds

These diamonds can be drafted in different proportions. As you can see by the illustration below, by changing the ratio, you get short and wide half diamonds or long and thin diamonds. This could be a real help in fitting a border to a side with odd measurements.

Two different proportions

We suggest that you use templates with the points trimmed to fit together the units for this border.

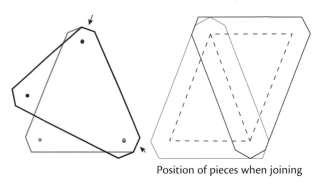

Position of pieces when joining

ALTERNATING DIAMONDS

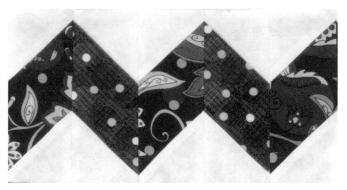

We have dealt with the math in this chapter with word problems and associations, not algebra. When dealing with diamonds, however, algebra may help you. This border is really based on the eight-pointed star, or LeMoyne Star. You can see where the shape is coming from in the following illustration of an eight-pointed star.

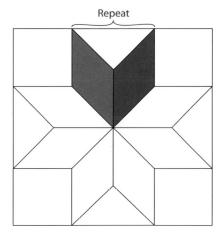

Repeat

The previous two diamond borders are easier to work with, as the measurements are straightforward. However, when the diamonds are tilted to the side, the drafting is more difficult. Now we need to deal with real math. If you didn't work through the drafting of eight-pointed stars in *Quilter's Academy Vol. 4*, Class 440 (pages 49–51), now would be a good time to learn this. Method 2 allows you to draft a star in any size you need. This will help with the algebra coming up.

Not being good at algebra, I turned to Jinny Beyer's book *Medallion Quilts* to get a specific answer to drafting and fitting this particular border. If I want the star points in the corners, how do I find out what size to make the diamonds? Her example uses a given size of 42″ × 69″. After dividing several different numbers to find a number of repeats that might work, she found the unit repeat number of 4.245 the best she could do. That would be 9.88 units on the 42″ side and 16.23 units on the 69″ side. With some fitting and adjusting, that could work. However, how do you draft a diamond the correct size to use in a 4.25″ unit? We can't work with graph paper, as that would give us parallelograms. So she suggests we draft an eight-pointed star into any size square you choose. In her example, she drafted an 8½″ square, which gave a distance of 3½″ across the triangle, which is where the measurement for the distance of the repeat unit comes from. Here is the equation to get this answer to accommodate the 4.25″ needed size.

We can now say that 3.5″ is to an 8½″ square as 4.25″ is to x″.

$$\tfrac{3}{5} - \tfrac{8}{5} = \tfrac{4}{25} - x$$

Work with this equation:

$3.5x = 8.5 \times 4.25$

$3.5x = 36.125$

$x = 10.32$ (this comes from dividing 36.125 by 3.5)

Now we know that an eight-pointed star will have to be drafted in a 10.32″ (10⅜″) square in order to get the correct sized pattern pieces. You can see that even this is not exact, as rounding up is necessary to work with a ruler.

This same procedure can be used for other eight-pointed star designs, like the diamond border we just covered—Diamonds at Attention. Once you figure out the repeat

distance (or the width of each star, in this case 1.5″) you need, fit it into the formula. An 8.5″ star would produce a diamond that is 1⅞″ across its widest point. Therefore, 1⅞″ is to an 8.5″ star as 1.5″ is to x″.

$$1\tfrac{7}{8} - \tfrac{8}{5} = \tfrac{1}{5} - x$$

$1.875x = 8.5 \times 1.5$

$1.875x = 12.75$

$x = 6.8$ (12.75 divided by 1.875)

You would need to draft the star in a 6.8″ square in order to get a diamond that was 1.5″ across.

We realize that most of you are blown away by this kind of math, as we often are. We do find, however, that when you sit down in quiet and work the equation repeatedly with different sizes, you start to see the logic in the whole thing. The answers derived from this type of drafting and math often result in needing to use templates if the measurements aren't ruler friendly, eliminating speed strip piecing. If all else fails, the way around this situation is to add small plain borders to grow the quilt top to a size that works with strip piecing measurements. We will attempt to address this again in *Volume 6*, which will be the PhD year.

When scouring dozens of quilt books to find ways to draft and construct borders, I was surprised that I couldn't find anything but charts of measurements that were in happy sizes, but no instructions as to how to make special sizes for odd measurements. If I wanted to develop a specific width border, or needed a specific repeat to fit the measurements of a given round of borders, it was nowhere to be found. Not being as sharp as we would like to be with math, we set out to actually do the math and see what happens. Here is our journey.

The edge of the quilt top that we want this border on measures 26.25″. After dividing even unit measurements into this number, the only one close was a repeat of 2″, but that only makes the border width come to about 2½″. That is too small for the appearance it would have on the quilt top. If the repeat was 3.25″, eight repeats would fit great, and it is an even number of pairs, so the corners would turn. Now what?

If we use the algebraic equation, we get the following:

$$\tfrac{3}{5} - \tfrac{8}{5} = \tfrac{3}{25} - x$$

$$3.5x = 8.5 \times 3.25 = 27.625$$

$$27.625 \div 3.5 = 7.89$$

$$x = 7.89 \text{ or } 7\tfrac{7}{8}$$

So next, we need to draft a 7⅞″ eight-pointed star.

Using the instructions from *Quilter's Academy Vol. 4*, Method 2 (page 50), draw a 7⅞″ square.

Work through all the steps to get the finished star. This should give us the center unit and the diamond size we need for our border, and to our surprise it was exact once the star was drafted.

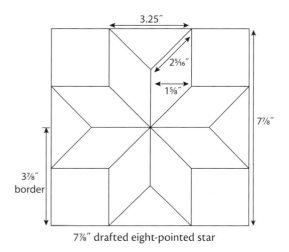

7⅞″ drafted eight-pointed star

Measure the width of the points, the length of one side of a point, and the distance between two points. Here are our answers:

The point is 1⅝″ wide.

The side of the point is 2⁵⁄₁₆″ long.

The distance between two points is 3¼″.

We then copied one of the design elements and drew them on a fresh sheet of graph paper to create the border.

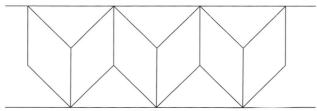

The border drawn from the star unit

Now all that is left is to draw in the lines that represent the strips of background and diamond fabric for strip piecing.

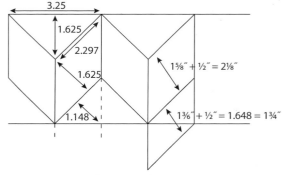

Getting the strip width measurements

We now know that the background strips are 1³⁄₁₆″. The way we know this is that the background strip has to accommodate the background triangle. If we know that the distance between the star points is 3¼″, the height of the triangle is 1⅝″. Multiply 1.625″ by 1.414 to get 2.297″ (the distance between the triangle point and the star point). This is also the length of each side of the star. The height of this small triangle is half of 2.297″, or 1.149″, or 1³⁄₁₆″. Add ½″ for seam allowances and you get 1.648″, or close to 1¾″. The diamond strip is 1⅝″, or 2⅛″ cut.

Because the diamonds mirror each other and generally are made of two different colors, you will need two different strip sets. The strip sets will be cut at opposite angles to one another. Iron seam allowances toward the center strip on one set and out toward the background on the second strip set. Remember to trim before adding the third strip.

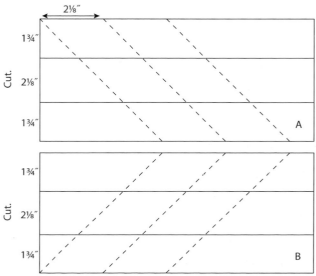

Strip sets A and B with angle of cuts

Once the segments are cut, sew one of each set together to form pairs and continue until your border is the right length. Iron seam allowances carefully to one side or open. Trim long sides, leaving ¼" for seam allowances.

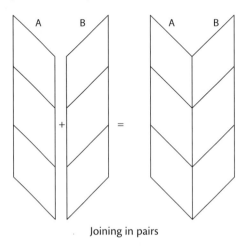

Joining in pairs

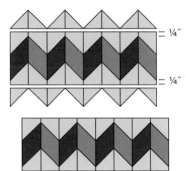

Trimming edges

Looking at the finished product, you see that we once again have the seam down the center of the side triangles because of the strip piecing method. If this is not pleasing to you because of the distraction the line can cause when quilting, or it is not true to the era of the quilt you are making, we can piece these units together using Y-seams as we do for constructing a LeMoyne Star.

Y-seam border

The first step of making a LeMoyne Star is to join two diamonds with a side triangle. These units make the border. These pieces can be cut with rotary measurements or templates if you had to draft a non–ruler friendly eight-pointed star for size. Trim the corners with the Corner Trimmer before you start to sew.

You will construct as many Y-units as you need per border, then join them together with triangles. Be sure to sew to the seamline only when you join the Y-units together so the triangle can be set into the point.

Start by laying out the three pieces needed for the units to the right of your machine. Stack as many units on top of one another as you need.

The Y-unit we are making

Pick up the triangle on the top of the pile and place it on the left diamond, right sides together. Align the edges and corners exactly. This is where the Corner Trimmer saves the day. Stitch the two pieces together with the triangle on top. This seam is stitched edge to edge.

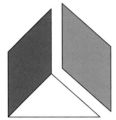

Stitch triangle to left diamond.

Do not clip threads or cut units apart. Continue to chain stitch the remaining units in the two piles until they are all joined. Clip the units apart and iron each seam allowance toward the diamond. Return the units to the same position they were in before sewing, where the remaining diamond is.

Pick up one of the units you just completed and place the right diamond on the top of the pile, right sides together with the triangle, again aligning the points of both exactly and making sure the edges are perfectly even.

Adding second diamond

Turn the unit over so that the triangle is on top and you can see the previously sewn seam. Sew from the edge of the triangle to the stitching and stop. Be careful not to go one stitch beyond the stitching.

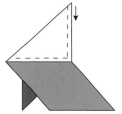

Sewing from triangle side

Continue until all units are joined. Iron seam allowances toward the triangle.

Next, fold one unit in half, right sides together, and align the edges of the diamonds. The triangle will be folded in half. Be sure that the points of the diamonds and the triangles, as well as all the outside edges, are even. Pin in place if you feel the need to hold the layers together tightly.

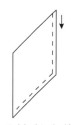

Folded in half

Pull the seam allowance down and out of the way before sewing. Sew this seam from the outer edge of the diamond point down to the previous stitching. Repeat with all remaining units. Iron seam allowance toward the left diamond (looking at the right side), ironing from the right side of the fabric.

Lay out the units to make the border length and place the remaining triangles. You will continue with the process you just completed, adding in the same manner the triangle that is not in place yet. Position the triangle on top of the left diamond and sew the seam end to end. Iron the seam toward the diamond. Position the triangle onto the next unit. With the triangle on top, stitch to the stitched seam. Iron the seam allowance toward the triangle.

Fold the two units in half and align all the seams. Stitch the diamonds together. Repeat until all the units are joined.

Join two Y-units, sewing from the triangle edge and stopping at the seamline where the two diamonds meet. Iron seam allowance to one side. Position the triangle in the opening and lay it on top of one of the diamonds, right sides together, aligning all the edges and the points exactly. Stitch to the stitching you just completed. Iron, and then flip the unit over and attach the opposite side of the triangle. Iron again. If everything aligned properly, you will have a ¼″ seam allowance beyond all the edge points for your border.

Backside of completed units

This would be a great border if it was scrappy, and this technique would easily accommodate the fabric changes.

DELECTABLE MOUNTAINS

We have added a few illustrations of Delectable Mountains borders. These designs show up in many of the nineteenth-century medallion quilts and are quite striking.

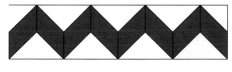

Units are positioned end to end.

Each mountain ends with separate triangles.

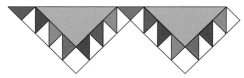

Units are sharing a triangle.

Horizontal seamed half-square triangle instead of vertical

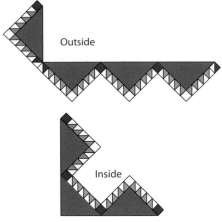

Outside

Inside

Inside and outside corner designs

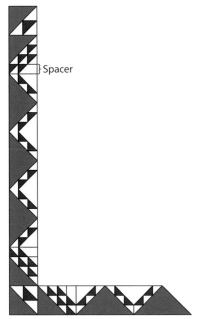

} Spacer

Unusual spacing at corners makes nice turn.

LOG CABIN

The use of Log Cabin blocks in borders makes a great outside or inside frame.

Log Cabin framing border

Log Cabin zigzag border

JAZZY NEW-STYLE BORDERS

We have included a few more modern-looking borders to jazz up your quilts.

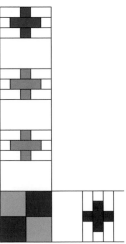

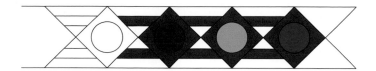

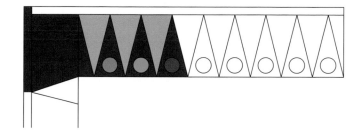

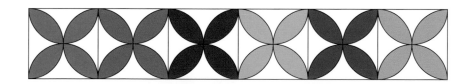

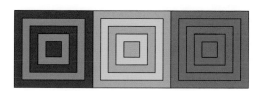

Gallery of modern-style borders

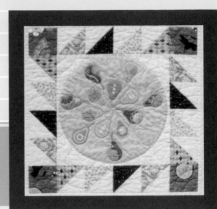

Going It Alone

If you made one or more of the more difficult quilts in this book, you have no doubt learned an amazing number of tricks, tips, and problem-solving solutions in the designing and construction of a quilt. We sincerely hope that you are at a point now so there is no intimidation about making any quilt you see or can dream up. Your toolbox has been filled with invaluable skills that make you a master quilter.

To finish the work and get your master's degree, your thesis is to create an original medallion quilt. We have provided you with a few line-drawn templates to get you started. You can fill in the blanks of any of them and set off to constructing it or use them as a platform for jumping into an original design. Either way, you have a blank piece of paper and a brain full of skill. We have no doubt you will create something wonderful. Congratulations on all your hard work.

Congratulations!

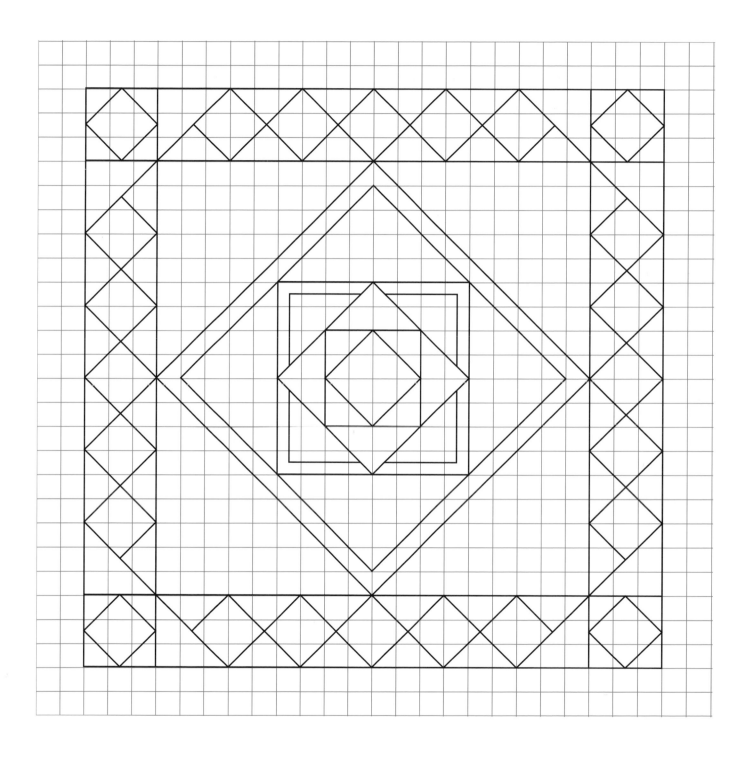

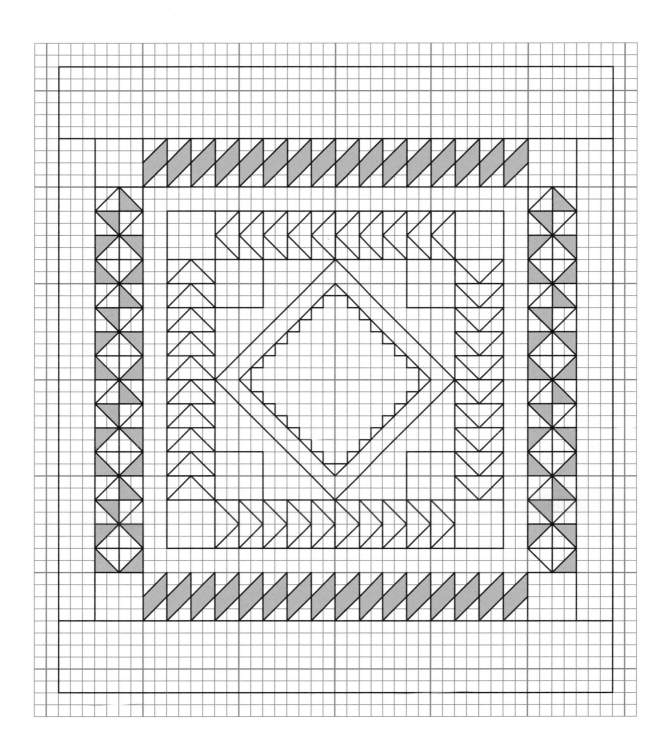

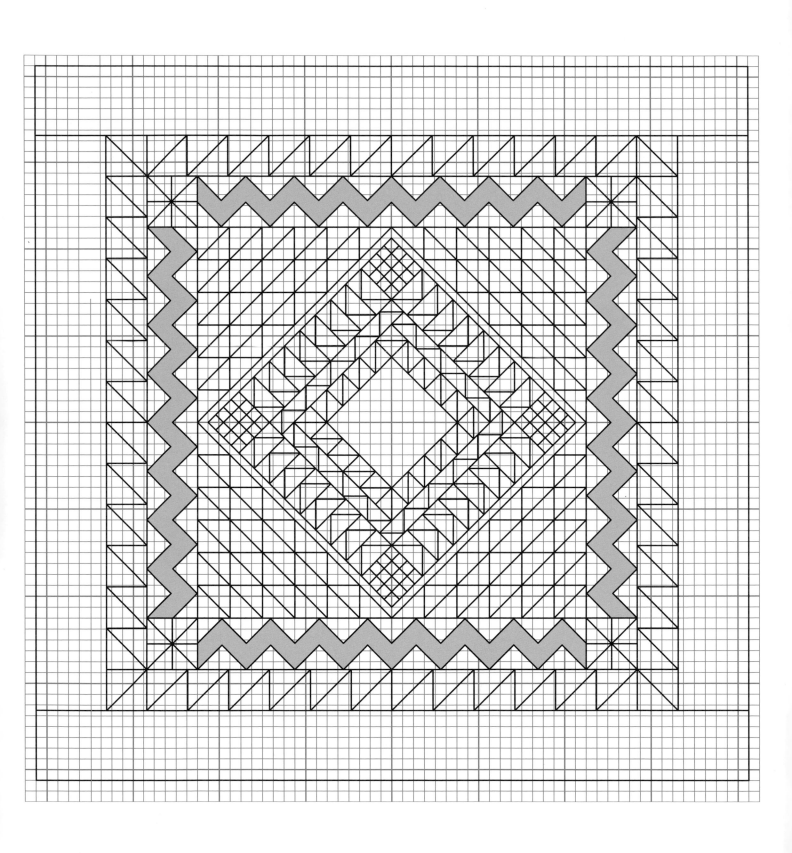

About the Authors

Harriet started quilting seriously in 1974, working alongside her mom. Her early quilting career included producing baby quilts for craft shows and teaching adult education classes. In 1981, Harriet opened her quilt shop, Harriet's Treadle Arts. Her specialties at the time were free-motion embroidery, machine arts, and machine quilting.

In 1982, Harriet attended one of Mary Ellen Hopkins's seminars. Mary Ellen's streamlined techniques and innovative design ideas led Harriet to a new way of thinking, which caused her to give up the machine arts and to teach only quilting. Today, she is world renowned for being a true "mover and shaker" in the quilt world. In the late 1990s, she was voted one of the "88 Leaders of the Quilt World."

Harriet created and inspired a whole new generation of machine quilters with her best-selling book *Heirloom Machine Quilting*, which has enjoyed 25 continuous years in print. She is also the author of *Mastering Machine Appliqué* and *From Fiber to Fabric*, and coauthor of *The Art of Classic Quiltmaking*. She is responsible for a myriad of products pertaining to machine quilting, and she has developed batting with Hobbs Bonded Fibers and designed fabric for P&B Textiles and Marcus Brothers.

Carrie has been around quilting all her life—sitting in Harriet's lap as a baby while Harriet sewed, learning her colors with machine embroidery thread and her alphabet on the cams of Harriet's old Viking sewing machine. She didn't have a chance not to be involved! Harriet and her mother opened the store when Carrie was four years old, and Carrie spent a part of nearly every day of her life at the store. Carrie's interests in college turned to range management and wildlife biology, but no matter what, she always came home to quilting as a hobby.

In 2006, Harriet decided she wanted to close the store. She was tired after running it for 25 years, as well as traveling and teaching at the same time. Carrie couldn't imagine not having the store as a part of her life. So she moved back to Colorado and now runs the store full time.

Most of all, Carrie is proud to carry on the family legacy of quilting that extends from her great-great-grandmother Phoebie

Frazier to her great-grandmother Harriet Carey to her grandmother Harriet (Fran) Frazier to her mom, Harriet. Quilting is all about tradition (no matter how you make a quilt) and about the love of creating something beautiful from fabric and thread with your own hands.

All the quilts in the book were pieced and quilted by Harriet and Carrie. They truly believe that if you are going to teach it, you had better be able to make it!

Resources

SUPPLIES/ SOURCE LIST

All notions and supplies referred to in the text are available from the following:

Harriet's Treadle Arts
6390 West 44th Avenue
Wheat Ridge, CO 80033
303-424-2742
harrietstreadlearts@zoho.com
harriethargrave.com

Information on Harriet's classes and retreats can be found on her website.

If you are looking for copies of Harriet's out-of-print books referred to in the text, they are available through C&T as eBooks and as POD (Print-On-Demand) Editions. Go to ctpub.com and search by author name to purchase.

Other titles by Harriet Hargrave: